FAIR
OR
FOUL?

The Complete Guide To Soccer Officiating

SIXTH EDITION

Harris & Harris

ACKNOWLEDGMENTS

The American Youth Soccer Organization
Arturo Angeles
Ken Aston
Ray Bernabei (NISOA)
Keith Cooper (FIFA)
Mario Donnangelo
Wes Dusek
Judy Embry (AYSO)
John Enroth (AYSO)
Federation Internationale de Football Association (FIFA)
The late Sam Foulds
Cynthia Harris (and Lucky)
Abraham Klein
Bill Mason
John Ouellette (AYSO)
Harry Rodgers
Doug Semark (AYSO)
Kitt Simeone (USYSA)
Bob Wertz (USSF)
Don Wilbur (USSF)
United States Youth Soccer Association
United States Soccer Federation

And finally, to soccer referees everywhere, thank you. We're all learning together.

Century Composing and Barbara Kendall.................Typesetting and Production Art
Chris Charney.. Various Art Work
Ron Davies .... Referee Characters
Les Jones/Judy Rauliuk of Covershots, Inc..Cover Photo
Robert Lovy ....Cover Design

ISBN 0-916802-25-6
Printed in the U.S.A.

DEDICATION

There is no longer a shortage of quality referee instructors at the national, state, or local level, and this is in great measure due to the selfless efforts of Ken Aston. His name stands alone today as an inspiration to all referees, just as it has for more than thirty years. While many international referees retire to memories of great occasions, Ken continues to usher new generations into the officiating side of the real "football."

Ken has known the game at every level. Still involved in "Schoolboy" soccer after more than six decades, he was first a player and later a coach of a team that was undefeated for five years running. For many years he officiated in the Football League, first as a linesman, then as referee, a career which culminated with his assignment to the Final at Wembley Stadium in London in 1963. One year earlier he was a referee at the World Cup in Chile, capping an 8 year career as an international referee.

A new level of commitment revealed itself in the mid-1960's, when he became a Member, then Deputy Chairman, and finally Chairman of the FIFA Referees' Committee. Still later, he was a member of the International Board and a Chief Instructor of Referees for FIFA.

A self-proclaimed highlight of Ken's soccer life has been his continued association with the American Youth Soccer Organization (AYSO), where he is Chief Instructor in the referee camps that bear his name. "I have seen AYSO grow from a young sapling to a strong and resilient tree, a magnificent testimony to the care and love of countless volunteers. I hope that I have made a contribution to this positive growth," he said from his home in Ilford, Essex, near London.

Whether it is a fine point of the Laws, in answering a query on the state of the current game, or a story to break the tension and frustration of an unresolved topic, Ken always manages to come through. "It is the human side, the spirit of the game and its Laws which always comes from his lips, and always with a smile," said a close observer of the wit, wisdom, and personality of soccer's friend and the world's #1 mentor of referees, Ken Aston.

Lastly, we pay tribute to the loving contributions and support of Ken's partner in life, Hilda. You have both helped us to meet the challenges and to experience the true joy of officiating in the world's greatest game. Thank you.

KEN ASTON'S PHILOSOPHY
The referee's job is to assure the maximum enjoyment of everyone present.

Ken and Hilda Aston

INTRODUCTION
TO THE SIXTH EDITION

Welcome to the new world of soccer! We hope you like our new format. Since the last edition we have all experienced a vast array of changes in our game. Most referees feel that these alterations to the Laws have been positive, and we agree. Also, World Cup '94 sent us all home with a mandate: "Enforce the Laws!" Though there were more cautions than before, there was more playing time, and what a show it was. Clearly, many lessons were learned from the 1990 World Cup, and the referees and linesmen delivered for FIFA and for the world in 1994.

The winds of change favor open, elegant, almost "virtuous" soccer, and the referees have a vital part in it all. Here are some ideas for you to contemplate for the immediate future:

1. Referees must strongly identify with the match. They are to be noticed. Boldly and prominently, they are to represent the spirit of the game, and not merely be the custodians of the Laws.
2. Referees represent authority, and this usually begins with the moment of truth in the match. This moment must be expected, and dealt with expeditiously. Leave no doubt as to who's in charge.
3. Referees must respond immediately to even minor problems of unsporting behavior. We have all seen it. For example, a player realizes that the throw-in or ball over the goal-line is not awarded in his favor, and he fails to pick it up for the opponent, who is much farther away. Deal with the situation then and there, and make sure that everyone around you hears your admonishment.

Fair or Foul is not a book on the Laws of the Game, but a reference and a guide for you as you progress. No longer containing the Laws, it is a companion to provide you with authority and direction.

As before, we encourage you to be consistent, decisive, courageous and honest. Be human. Remember that you're more than a referee. You are an ambassador of the game. Many people depend on you and on an earnest performance. We're with you.

Assessing and being assessed is only one part of your education, which should never end.

SIR STANLEY ROUS
1895-1986

The 100th anniversary of the birth of Stanley Rous brings a renewed awareness of his immense contributions to soccer. A personification of English soccer for more than 50 years, he was a deep thinker and later a man of great influence worldwide. As an international referee, he was once feted by FIFA for reffing "in a large manner". His breadth of vision brought the first coaching schools, a decision he later regretted. ("Too much instruction.") He never  wavered in his support for and interest in refereeing. His first act as Secretary of the Football Association (F.A.) in 1934 was to have a medal struck for those who officiated in F.A. Cup Final games. He codified and rewrote the Laws of the Game, and developed the Diagonal System of Control. As President of FIFA for 13 years, he brought the modern game to an appreciative world. For all of his accomplishments, Rous was best known for his integrity in all matters.

At the famous Colombes Stadium in Paris, 1930. Where are the linesmen? We're not sure. This was prior to his Diagonal System of Control.

THE QUOTABLE ROUS...

"Soccer is a game, under whatever label it may be played."

"It is so easy to think a change in the Laws can brighten a game when what is wanted is a change of player attitudes."

"One of the most important lessons is to respect the authority of the referee by accepting his decisions without dissent. Later in life, when a man finds himself as a judge of situations in daily work, he knows how to be fair to employees and colleagues."

THE SPIRIT OF THE GAME
by Ken Aston

Soccer (in case you didn't know!) is classed as a 'war game' in that the players attempt to "win" the opponents' citadel (goal). To be accurate, therefore, players 'win' goals and it is the referee who scores them in his notebook. In the old days, the woodwork of the goalposts was actually scored by a knife or hatchet when a goal was won at that end!

Just as wars are governed -- or should be -- by the internationally recognized Laws & Usages of War, so soccer is governed by Laws whilst the "Usages" are covered by the unwritten *Spirit of the Game*. For example, no matter how bitter the war, the Flag of Truce is always honored; if a player is obviously injured, an opponent will often kick the ball out of play so that he may get immediate attention. This is part of the *Spirit of the Game*, The Golden Thread, which harks back to the days when the game was played by "Gentlemen". Now Gentlemen don't cheat - they may well offend the Laws by ignorance of them, lack of skill, clumsiness, excitement, or over-exuberance, but never deliberately. The precious Golden Thread is sacrosanct. The younger the player in AYSO, the closer he or she is to the gentlemen who originally played the game.

It is vital that referees should have a real feeling and understanding of the Spirit, and to be alert to cut out anything which contravenes it. Further, it has always been my view that this "feel" for the Spirit must on occasions condition a referee's opinion and hence the decision on a particular incident. For example, the ball is crossed strongly from the winger chest-high across the goal-mouth; the striker is running at full speed to head it into the net; he misses it with his head but the ball strikes his hand as it pistons forward in his running action. The ball finishes in the back of the net. Deliberate "hands"? NO. An offense? NO. A good goal? NO! Why not? Because the Spirit of the Game overrides the letter of the Law and to allow a goal would be contrary to the very nature of the game, and the ensuing freekick would be accepted by everyone as being right. A word of warning, however -- never let your feeling for the Spirit become an excuse for not carrying out your duty as you know you should.

Soccer is a universal game, played in all countries at all levels and by both sexes. It is the game enjoyed by players of widely differing cultures, social and economic backgrounds, and very contrasting temperaments. Yet, it is very much a body-contact game played with comparatively few problems. Recent legislation and directives from FIFA and the International Board have done a great deal to re-establish the discipline of the game and the spirit of Fair Play after a period when both were at a low ebb. The greatest problem the game faces is the steady breakdown of social discipline and its unwelcome intrusion into soccer. Hopefully, the game can play its part in resolving the problem with its participants, for the game was originally designed by the schools not only for sport, recreation, and physical exercise, but to inculcate the disciplines of life. How to control excitement, frustration, disappointment, anger even. How to respect opponents, to work in a team, to be modest in victory and generous in defeat, to accept decisions you don't agree with, and to conduct yourself properly at all times. It is the referee who must do his or her best to see that players conform to these requirements for the total enjoyment of the game for all present.

MEET THE AUTHORS
Paul Harris and Larry Harris

PAUL HARRIS' soccer passion has kept him out of trouble for about fifty years. He played on championship teams in high school, college, and as a semi-professional.

For five years he was Director of Officiating for the American Youth Soccer Organization (AYSO), where he began the Referee Camps, conceived the TRIO program for evaluation, developed the PHield test and did some coaching. Later he became a linesman and later an assessor of referees for the North American Soccer League and the American Soccer League.

Author of 20 books on the game, his greatest soccer memory was spending 16 interrupted (by games) days on the roof of his house. The occasion was World Cup '94, and he remained there until the American team was eliminated.

His most difficult game of the more than 2000 he has officiated? "Once I was in the middle for a game of 'under 8' girls, just four blocks from my house. The fire engines raced by the field, and I could see the smoke from my neighborhood. I was convinced my house was burning down. I finished the game, and rushed home. It turned out that it was the same address as my home, but on the next block. Looking back, I didn't have full concentration throughout."

LARRY HARRIS is a Human Factors Scientist, specializing in individualized instruction and Computer Based Training. He has conducted seminars for instructional designers, umpires, scorekeepers, bridge directors/players as well as for soccer referees.

Larry officiated in the now-defunct American Soccer League (ASL) and was a NISOA collegiate referee for 20 years. He was the Southern California Soccer Officials Association Commissioner of Certification and President of the Los Angeles chapter for nine years.

As a bridge professional and Silver Life Master, he has won numerous regional, team and open championships. He also directs duplicate bridge tournaments on a regular basis.

In addition to *Fair or Foul?*, Larry has authored *Futbol Means Soccer*, *Score*, *Bridge Directors' Companion* and *Bridge Players' Companion*.

Larry Harris (left)
and Paul Harris

FIFA AND JOSEPH "Sepp" BLATTER

As General Secretary of Federation Internationale de Football Association (FIFA), "Sepp" Blatter has had a significant role in the development of the modern game. He has encouraged loftier standards of referee performance, not only in major competition, but in all games of FIFA's 191 member countries.

As we approach the 21st Century, Blatter's quest for a worldwide* application of the Laws is evident. Football is indebted to him, both for his leadership and his vision.

*Members of FIFA not Members of the United Nations:

Aruba
Cayman Islands
Chinese Taipei
Faeroe Islands
Hong Kong
Kampuchea
Macao
Puerto Rico
Switzerland (Observer status)
Tahiti

Due for 1996 Membership
Andorra
Guam
Palestine

FIFA's and my personal aim is to promote positive, attacking football and to better protect elegant, technically skilled players from fouls. Modifications such as the new ruling on tacklings or the amended off-side law bring this about.
Joseph Blatter

TABLE OF CONTENTS

In control, in command. Directing, managing, restraining, yet at the same time, letting them play. Sandor Puhl of Hungary at the Final in July 1994.
Photo by Les Jones/Judy Rauluik of Covershots, Inc.

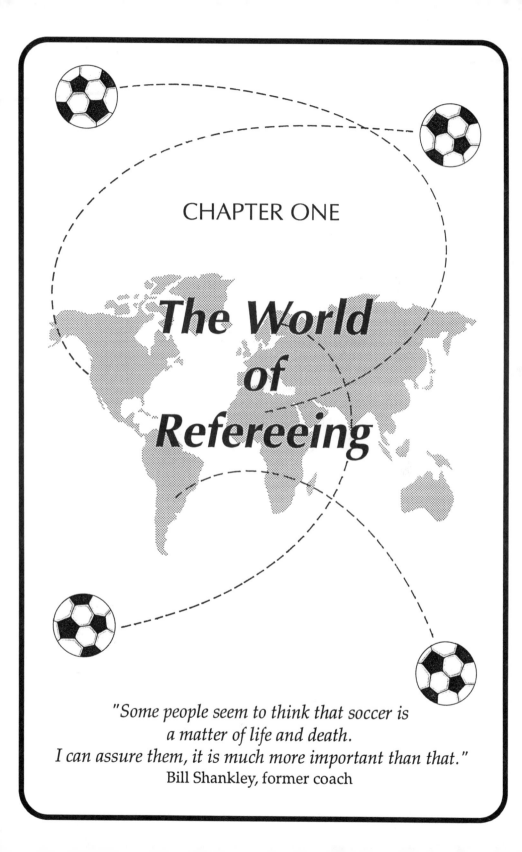

CHAPTER ONE

The World of Refereeing

*"Some people seem to think that soccer is
a matter of life and death.
I can assure them, it is much more important than that."*
Bill Shankley, former coach

IS REFEREEING FOR YOU?

Even as you read this, you may not be entirely convinced that refereeing is for you. If you have been recruited into a volunteer youth soccer organization, you will immediately know that there is more recognition elsewhere. Coaching, for instance has its larger rewards of team parties, parental support, and player adulation. If you are entering through your experience in officiating another sport, you may find that soccer has its own peculiarities, lore, war stories, and challenges.

The first time you walk on the field, you have immediately become a member of a very large but exclusive club, a worldwide group that has nearly 400,000 members. When you become a referee, you will never again see the game the same way. Immediately you will know more about the Laws than many successful coaches. You will view Law application in terms of dynamic play and the question of "Does it work?" will be changed to "Is it fair?". When you referee, you run the risk of being hooked. You will experience an exhilaration, a sense of well-being and self-confidence, a feeling that you are in control. It is a feeling that all is right with your world. In summary, it can change your life.

We must be totally honest with you about your task, for there are negative stories attached to soccer officiating. On any given day, a fair percentage of referees, while officiating, wish they were elsewhere. They are unsure of themselves, and have been intimidated, abused, or maligned in any number of ways. Potential referees on the sidelines view referees in trouble and decide "It's not worth it." At season's end about two in five referees will not return. "It's a thankless job," are words often heard.

From the moment you begin, one of your tasks will be to improve the position of referees in the game. We want you to be among the three referees in five who continue from one season to the next. Here are some personal guidelines for your own advancement in the world of soccer officiating:

1. **CHALLENGE YOURSELF.** As you become comfortable in one level of competition, move up.
2. **ASK FOR HELP.** Request a game observation from an experienced fellow official.
3. **LIMIT YOUR ACTIVITY.** Two regular games in a day is maximum. If you whistle more, you will lose concentration and effectiveness.
4. **RECOGNIZE YOUR FRAILTIES.** Know you make mistakes, but forget them, and go on. Einstein said, "Only death can release you from making blunders."
5. **SUPPORT OTHERS.** You will see others in predicaments. Help them by making suggestions, if asked.

ABOVE ALL, TAKE YOUR JOB SERIOUSLY, AND KEEP IMPROVING.

> **"Refereeing is Thinking."**
> *Ken Aston*

THE ECSTASY, THE ELATION, AND THE EXUBERANCE OF REFEREEING

"A room full of referees should be different from a room full of coaches. In one, there's competition. In another, there's cooperation."

The referee's world is very different. Fulfillment is...

KNOWING THAT

You can let kids be who they are.
No two games are ever the same.
You can handle anything.
There will be no game without you.
You can help other referees.
Some day you will get very close to calling the perfect game.

BEING ABLE TO

Remember your first game, with fondness.
Answer the 7-year-old's question, "Did we win?"
Be in control of yourself and of others.
Be right there when someone scores his first goal.
Learn something new each game.
Witness a tie game where everyone's happy.
Hear a coach with only positive encouragement.
Treat each game like a World Cup Final.
Blow the whistle and know that everyone will accept your decision.
Look at your partners and know that you each saw it the same way.
Hear the losing coach say, "You players are really improving."
Say, "I wish I could do that" to a player who has just done the "flip" throw-in.
Hear a teenager say, "How can I get to be a ref?"
Referee a game in a warm rain.

Referees have many opportunities for teamwork.

YOUR FITNESS FOR REFEREEING

It has been repeatedly observed that vast individual differences appear in referee dress, attitude, experience, and ability. Conditioning and training present no exception. Some referees train, almost religiously, for their task, yet others let the games provide the setting for their training.

If you are a fanatic for conditioning, don't try to outrun the ball, the players, or the play. Also, don't try to set a record by whistling nine games in a day, as at least one referee did. Conversely, if you take conditioning lightly, you will probably not progress very far in refereeing. So... what is a realistic approach to the physical task that is before you?

In an earlier edition of this book we stated that physical condition was 50% of refereeing. We still believe it is important. At best, it is 25%, and maybe only 15%. The referee who is confidently "in shape" will feel able to perform as well in the last minute as in the first. Other referees will find that as the game clock runs down, so will the physical clock. The demands made upon the referee are often greatest in the last minutes of the game, with frustrated players and desperate, fatigued, less-than-fully-coordinated moves by all.

Officials in various sports will find varying demands made upon them, depending on the game itself. The realities of your job will tell you that:

- You will spend a great deal of your time moving at medium speed, at a slow, easy trot, at 60% efficiency.
- At least ten times in a game you must run full-speed, for 30 yards or more, to view a quick attack on goal.
- Much of your effective running must be backwards or sideways.
- You must have mobility to avoid players and the ball.
- Even the shortest game is usually stopped at least 50 times for throw-ins, goal-kicks, corner-kicks, free-kicks, goals, injuries, substitutions, etc. Don't let anyone tell you that soccer is continuous. When you do have these breaks in play, don't rush into your next position. Save your strength.

Lest you feel complacent, thinking that the job is not physically demanding, the following chart is offered:

	Referee	Linesmen
Diagonal System	6 - 7 miles	2 - 3 miles
Modified Diagonal	5 - 6 miles	3 - 4 miles
One Referee System	8 - 10 miles	⚽

These distances refer to the amount of "moving about" that an average referee would do in a normal 90 minute game, and would, of course, be dependent on the size of the field.

Referees are athletes. Ingrid Jonsson of Sweden in full stride deep on the diagonal: USA 3, China 3.

A recent FIFA report on WC'94 indicates the following:

Distance covered in Game

Referee- 12,600 meters (7.8 *miles*)

Midfielder-11,300 meters (7.0 *miles*)

Forward - 9,500 meters (5.9 *miles*)

HINTS

1. *Before the game, run from one goal to the other to inspect the nets. This effort will "warm you up" in cool weather and will impress both players and spectators with your enthusiasm and alertness.*

2. *A ball travels faster than any player or referee can run. Keep up with the play, not with the ball.*

3. *Prior to the opening of the regular season, ask league officials for practice game assignments. This will aid in both mental and physical conditioning.*

4. *Through experience you will learn to avoid unnecessary running on the field, thus saving your energies for sudden breakaways on goal when you must not be caught too far behind play.*

5. *Never lean on a goal upright during a game stoppage.*

6. *Use the half time period for rest and for game discussion with your fellow officials.*

EQUIPMENT

"When the occasion is worth dressing for, it's worth the best in dress."

The most obvious part of a referee's equipment is his uniform, which should consist of the following:

1. *A long or short sleeved black shirt, with white collar and cuffs, with the crest of the referee's association on the left side of the chest.*
2. *Black shorts, with length 4 to 5 inches above the knees.*
3. *Black stockings, with white or white stripes at the top.*
4. *Black studded shoes, with black or white shoe laces.*

It is recommended that a transparent or black waterproof jacket be worn in rainy weather. A black visor/cap helps protect the referee who wears glasses from the rain. It is also handy as a sun shade. When it is determined that one team's colors are in conflict with the standard black of the referee, the referee shall change to a shirt of contrasting color or pattern. A fuchsia colored shirt, as first seen in WC '94, and the basic referee shirt with the black and white reversed are two popular alternatives.

The referee's equipment must also include a referee data card or a small pocket notebook and the following:

Whistles (2)   Coin
Watches (2) (one must have stop action)   Red and Yellow Cards (1 set)
Pencils (2)

Many referees have the following items in their equipment bag:

Glasses with yellow lenses   Increases contrast and visibility for games played at night, in rain, fog, or when very overcast.

Spare set of red and yellow cards
Law Book
Set of linesman's flags
Shoe polish
Spare pair of shoes   Screw-in cleats are best for a wet field.
Inflating pump and valve needle
36" of a cloth tape measure
Shoe laces -- black and white   A spare pair. If you function as a linesman, you can change to match the referee.

String/cord and a knife   For the emergency repair of nets.
Masking/Adhesive tape   To repair nets and to hold up ones stockings.
Captains' arm bands
Screw-in cleat tool
Band-aids and chapstick
File for burrs on cleats, etc.

LESS FLAK FOR THE ONES IN BLACK!

If proper field execution is what we all must strive for, perhaps now is the time to reflect upon our strong and weak points.

The diagram below depicts that there are five major ingredients necessary for the fully prepared referee. Before considering these five ingredients, let's first examine the largest barrier for the referee who wishes to successfully implement these tools. The barrier is, of course, **ATTITUDE**. Attitude colors, distorts, and enhances all that we do on the field.

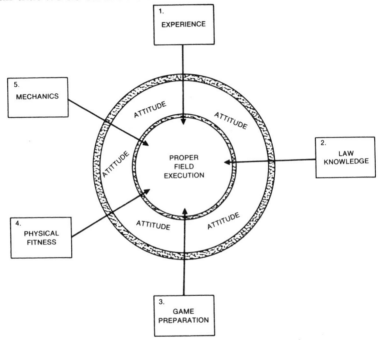

THE TEN COMMANDMENTS OF ATTITUDE

Review the following commandments regularly. They are every bit as important as the rules contained within FIFA's Laws of the Game.

1. *Thou shalt have a good image* -- What do you convey to the players, coaches, and spectators?... Do you look the part?... Are cards hanging out of your pockets?... Socks at half-mast?... Ill-fitting uniform?... Are you viewed as a little Caesar or a Casper Milktoast?

2. *Thou shalt have rapport with fellow officials* -- How do you appear to your partners? Are you capable of putting them at ease? Do you bring out the best in them? If you don't, it's possibly *your* fault.

3. *Thou shalt concentrate* -- Are you able to sustain concentration throughout the game? Do you totally dedicate yourself to the task at hand for a full 90 minutes or do you occasionally find yourself standing around just watching play? How successful are you in fighting off mental fatigue? Most referees find that to do

more than one or two games in a day results in attention loss. When doing multiple games, are you with it or just a body putting in time? Don't accept too heavy a load. It does the game a disservice. If you must do it in a tournament... try to pace yourself.

4. *Thou shalt be emotionally stable* -- We have all seen the symptoms of instability on the field. The referee who appeared in house slippers to officiate a college game. He told a coach at halftime that he would beat him up if he received a bad rating... The referee who was red-lined ("Do not assign") by all six of the schools within a particular high school league because he was so abrasive... The referee who gets players and coaches upset even before the game has started. The unstable referee is not disciplined.

5. *Thou shalt be self-disciplined* -- Can you control yourself on the field? Do you overreact to abuse? Do you intelligently apply the laws in a calm, professional manner?

6. *Thou shalt have confidence in self* -- Do you think well of yourself? Do you like you?... Don't overdo it though, the flipside of the coin is being pompous and on an ego trip. The confident referee is not defensive.

7. *Thou shalt be non-defensive* -- Are you able to be self-effacing? Can you admit your mistakes? (Where, when, how, and to whom is another matter)... or is it always 'them' (players, coaches, spectators, or partners)? By his actions, the non-defensive referee exudes confidence.

8. *Thou shalt be motivated* -- Are you motivated to give your very best effort, regardless of the level of play? If not, don't work the game... even if you are donating your time.

9. *Thou shalt be flexible* -- Do you have the ability to modify your behavior?... or are you rigid, being unable to adapt to each new and unexpected situation as is occurs? Are you a good listener?

10. *Thou shalt not use the name of the referee in vain* -- How badly do you chew up the referee when you are functioning as a coach or a spectator? Do you discretely keep it to yourself or only for the ears of a close companion? Some referees are the most venomous critics imaginable. Why is this done?... Insecurity!!! Usually the weakest referees chip away at others. Normally the louder and more vicious they are, the poorer is their own officiating. To openly criticize is to expose your own weakness... and those of all the others in black.

THE FIVE MAJOR INGREDIENTS

1. *Experience* is the *most important* ingredient. Unfortunately it only comes with time. It takes much time to assimilate all that you have been exposed to. Often your very assignments are restrictive. You can't mature as an official if you never have difficult, challenging games. Seek out the potentially challenging games. It may be painful, but with the proper attitude, it will aid your growth. Vicarious experience can be gained from watching other referees in action. Empathize with them during the game. What can you learn from them? What could they have learned from you?

2. *Law Knowledge* links up very closely with experience. You can't be a quality referee without knowing the Laws cold. You can, however, know the Laws inside and out and be quite ineffective on the field. A frequently heard put-down of a referee by a fellow official is: "He is no good because he is a book referee." Although this statement is often true, it seems to always come from a speaker who is attempting to justify *his* less than adequate knowledge of the Laws. The same parallel can be drawn between him and the referee who magnifies the ineptness of another official. The 'book referee' statement is particularly offensive because it demeans one's essential knowledge of the Laws of the Game.

3. *Game Preparation* -- Do you mentally prepare for all your games? How much do you learn about the teams before you referee? Do you know how to handle situations before they occur? Or do you just walk onto the field and slide into the match? It's no problem if the game doesn't test you, but if it does, you could be challenged in ways you didn't expect.

4. *Physical fitness* is a neglected part of many referees' regimen. Many referees use their games as a conditioning tool, complacently moving from one assignment to the next. A conscientiously fit referee considers pre-season, season, and post-season fitness. The game requires up to ninety minutes of physical effort, with up to 7 miles of jogging, sprinting, walking, back-pedaling and side-stepping. Only you know before a game if you are prepared in body and in mind. As the game progresses, others will know as well.

5. *Mechanics* -- A well-known referee assessor recently said, "Of all the sports I've observed, soccer officials are the worst in mechanics." Unfortunately he is right. The importance of mechanics has been recognized by various local high school officials' associations. Football and basketball tests have 25-30% of their test items devoted to mechanics. The baseball association allocates approximately 35% of its qualification exam to this important area. Mechanics should be learned so that it becomes reflexive in nature. Deviation from the 'accepted' is fine as long as you have a very good reason for doing so... other than being lazy or having a lack of mental concentration.
   Mechanics is the link between game tactics and game control.

There is absolutely no excuse for having deficiencies in either Law knowledge or mechanics because they are static, and can be studied out of a book. Wouldn't it be nice if we could gain experience in the same manner?

You may ask the question, "How can I gain a noticeable improvement in my soccer officiating skills in the shortest period of time?"... the answer for the majority would be... STUDY MECHANICS!!!

Q: One player seems to be bearing the brunt of the opponents' fouls, and has been fouled five times, each time by a different player. Can "persistent infringement" be applied here? How?
A: *No, a caution for persistent infringement is given to a player who has persisted in infringing the Laws of the Game.*

ABRAHAM KLEIN...
Both Mentally and Physically...
He's Always Ready

Each year, Abraham Klein makes a special journey to the Dallas Cup competition in Texas. It's about half a world away from his home in Haifa, Israel, but the former FIFA referee is pleased to be part of the most international of youth soccer tournaments.

"Officiating a youth game is no different from a World Cup Final. Anything can happen. Players, coaches and the fans all expect your best. I prepare the same for both levels of competition."

Klein, a physical educator, whose son, Amit, received his FIFA badge in January 1995, has had his share of responsibilities in the middle. Now a veteran of three FIFA World Cups and two Olympics, he met the challenge of his life on June 7, 1970. Defending champion England bowed, 1-0, to eventual champion Brazil, in one of soccer's historic end-to-end struggles. It helped set the standard for FIFA's greatest spectacle of positive soccer. Unbelievably, not one player was sent off in the month-long competition.

Abraham Klein is a keen student of the game, and no referee has been better prepared, physically and mentally, for the demands of world-class play. Whether it's stress-release, training for strength, endurance or speed, even nutrition for the ascending referee, Klein is passionate and dedicated. He now helps others become the best they can be, and is an inspector of games for UEFA in Europe.

His credentials are impeccable, and his refereeing talents have been recognized on every continent. During the World Cup '94 in the United States, he was especially pleased to see players from youth teams he had whistled now representing their countries at the greatest of all soccer events. Abraham still referees every week in youth games in Israel. His advice to referees everywhere: "Have your own tactical plan, know the players and the teams, and be on top of every situation."

During the 1982 FIFA World Cup. A major struggle between Italy and Brazil. Klein is right on top of the play.

GITTE LYNGØ NIELSEN
of Copenhagen, Denmark

Gitte Nielsen is used to success. For seven years she played for a team named "Fortuna", Danish national champion in 1994. However, now she has time only for officiating; which she has been doing since 1988. "Almost all of my vacations and spare time is spent on being a referee or lineswoman," says the 25-year-old pharmacist. "It's the only way to get better. Here at home I'm in the best women's competition, and also officiate the men's games."

Gitte is very competitive, and now that she is no longer a player, she's competing with herself, and is well-rewarded. Before she was nominated to FIFA's elite list, she officiated in Sweden, Norway, Finland, Portugal, and Cyprus. And, no red cards in her international career to date! "But, I've stopped counting them in national games," Gitte adds, with her winning smile.

WOMEN REFEREES AND LINESWOMEN LISTED BY FIFA

In late January of 1995, FIFA announced its first provisional list of Women Referees and Lineswomen. Thirty-one lineswomen from twenty-two FIFA member countries were listed, as well as thirty-one referees from twenty-three different nations.

Many of these women earned the FIFA badge by officiating in international games of women players, and most played soccer in their countries. With these nominations for the FIFA list comes an expectation that women's soccer has come of age in many of FIFA's 191 countries and that women officials will be respected as leaders in game management.

The "flip-throw" seems to be an American phenomenon, just as the "bicycle" kick was introduced by the Brazilians. Rob Johnson (above) of Rutgers University. "To the opposition, every "flip-throw" is a serious threat," says Johnson's coach, Bob Reasso. "And, the fans love it."

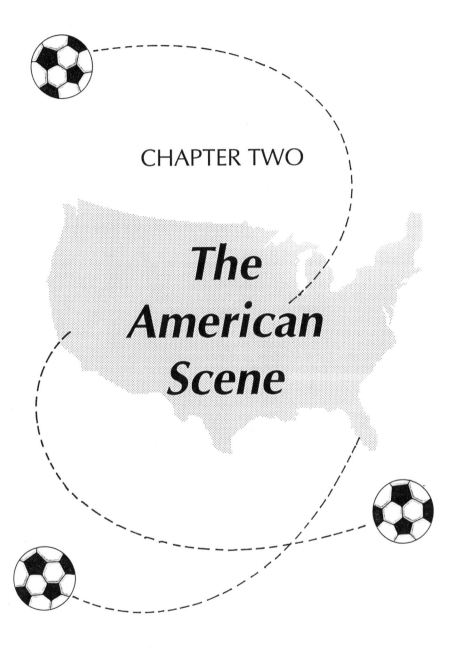

CHAPTER TWO

The American Scene

"Our vision is to become a pre-eminent worldwide model for referee excellence by the year 2005."
Bob Wertz, Chairman
National Referee Committee, United States Soccer Federation

THE AMERICAN YOUTH SOCCER ORGANIZATION...
Where "Everyone Plays"

The American Youth Soccer Organization (AYSO), a national affiliate member of The United States Soccer Federation, recently celebrated its 30th year of service to youth. With more than 500,000 players in 46 states and in Russia, AYSO's philosophy of "Everyone Plays" is at the very heart of the program. With all players, regardless of ability, taking part in at least half of every game, AYSO has set the standard not only for youth soccer, but for other youth sports as well.

Bill Hughes, a founder who still whistles in his home region of Palos Verdes, California, says, "There was very little out there for youngsters back in the early 1960's. We wanted to give everyone a chance to play this game that is open, fun, and which would attract parents as well." As it turns out, soccer certainly is a family activity. Bill would agree with AYSO's current leaders, who state the goals of the organization: "To provide positive child development through a fair, safe, and fun soccer environment."

A unique feature of the referee program at AYSO is that all of their 40,000 referees and linespersons are unpaid for their efforts. These volunteers, many of whom are also coaches, will vary in their commitment and experience. At the entry level are those who are linespersons or beginners who whistle games of "Under 8s", helping out at the regional level. At the National level are those who can be assigned to any game, including in any of AYSO's 100 tournaments or special games involving visiting foreign teams.

Referee Grades

Designation	Description	Number
Linesperson	New volunteers trained to run line in Divisions 7-5	7,000
Regional Referee	New volunteers trained to referee in Divisions 7 and up to Division 5	30,000
Area Referee	Experienced Regional Referees trained and promoted through Division 4	4,400
Section Referee	Experienced Area Referees trained and promoted through Division 3	1,000
National 2 Referee	Experienced Section Referees trained and promoted through Division 2	250
National 1 Referee	Experienced National 2 Referees trained and promoted through Division 1	300

Most regions (usually a community) require a candidate's attendance at an eight-hour clinic taught by a certified instructor. At this entry level, all candidates are presented with, and tested on, information required to control a match of "Under 8s". Regional, Area, and Section programs are overseen by Regional Referee Administrators, Area Referee Administrators, and Section Referee Administrators, respectively.

AYSO's National Referee Program is headed by a fulltime Director of Officiating, Doug Semark. Along with his counterpart in coaching, John Ouellette, Semark is constantly on the lookout for areas of cooperation between coaching and refereeing. Both of their Commissions agree that small-sided games, (often called Minisoccer), are the best way to introduce young players, coaches, parents, and referees to AYSO and its philosophy. Ouellette is a National 1 Referee, and frequently instructs in referee training courses. Semark has 17 years of coaching experience, and has conducted clinics for new coaches. Both Semark and Ouellette are committed to the basic "team objectives" of AYSO.

THE FIRST MEMORANDUM FOR MATCH OFFICIALS - 1886

"If players would always remember that when they are behind the ball, at the moment of kicking, they cannot be offside, but when they are in front of the ball, they are always liable to be offside, it would simplify the meaning of the Law very much."

DOUG SEMARK
AYSO's National Director of Officiating

"A lot of people seem to be thoroughly enjoying an extended childhood. Maybe we can help them along that worthy adventure."

As a youngster, Doug Semark went to Boy Scout Camp. Like many of his Ohio friends, he prayed it would never end. "It was a magical feeling, and I repeat that feeling with every game. As I see it, my job is to provide programs and leadership that will create that experience for many of our 40,000 referees."

You simply can't lure Doug into a lengthy discussion on the off-side or how to handle free-kicks near goal. He's much more interested in loftier topics, some of which are part of the training courses he's developed. "Players are impressionable. We encourage referees to be good role models, to use their authority in constructive ways, to show youngsters the way. Our programs are designed to bring people together. We also teach people to deal with resistance and anger. All of it is to turn every situation into something that is an exercise in discipline and character-building."

A surprise to many of the 4000 volunteers Doug meets every year is the depth of his officiating experience. Volleyball, basketball, football, track and field, even wrestling, fencing, and cross-country are part of his referee background. Soccer, however, has the simplest Laws, Doug believes. "To be in the middle of a soccer game is the ultimate, whatever one's age," he says. The role of young referees in youth soccer is one of his favorite topics. "They have more right to be on the field, doing their thing, on that day, than any adult. We're working hard to re-establish the rights of youth participants who are referees. These kids are a positive influence on their peers, and on the adult volunteers. Also, they make very good decisions during play."

Doug is AYSO's 7th Director of Officiating in its 31 years, and the first full-timer. Occasionally he shows up in a region and asks to run line or two. "It's at this level that I can see if our programs are working, and to experience first-hand how people are joining together for the youngsters." Many years ago, Doug discovered the joy inherent in the AYSO refereeing experience. From that day on, he decided to never again do a game for pay. "It was 17 years ago, and was a whole new experience. Amazingly, it was fun. The AYSO soccer environment was new life, the next best thing to playing the beautiful game. I'd have to say I've never done an AYSO game I didn't enjoy."

OBJECTIVE:	ACCOMPLISHED BY:	EFFECT ON PLAYERS:
Open Registration	No try-outs	No matter what the skill, any child can join AYSO.
Balanced Teams	Equalize player skill among the teams	Every team has a chance to score.
Everyone Plays	Substitution by quarters	Everyone plays at least half a game and for many kids, winning is getting to play.
Positive Coaching	Use positive comments that instruct and encourage	Kids develop a positive self-image when adults focus on the positives.
Good Sportsmanship	Use and teach sporting behavior	Adults and kids learn to be good sports by doing it.

The Diagonal System of Control is taught in all of AYSO's clinics, and most of the organization's 400,000 games each year are conducted under this FIFA-approved system. Referees are taught to interact positively and constructively with players, coaches, and parents. The safety and well-being of players is emphasized by coaches and referees alike.

The largest player registration for AYSO is in Division 5, where many referees begin their volunteering. Here, ball-sharing begins, players are learning about team play, and parents become more sensitive to the efforts of all in the AYSO "family."

For more than 20 years, AYSO has supported the interests of youngsters who choose to referee. Under a Director of Youth Programs, more than 5,000 boys and girls annually act as referees or linespersons. Though they are sometimes trained separately, as is true in the Youth Referee Camps, they are actively assimilated into the training programs for adult volunteers. The purpose of the youth program is to use soccer refereeing as a tool, emphasizing a set of values. Discipline, dependability, and honesty are stressed, along with a study of the Laws and of refereeing technique. "We want to counteract some negative forces in society, and give the young people a totally positive experience", Semark indicates, summing up the philosophy of having kids in charge of a kid's game.

The Referee Commission, headed by Semark, meets twice annually, with 18 members. All Section Referee Administrators are in membership, as well as Directors of Assessment, Administration, Instruction, Youth Programs, and the FIFA Law Interpreter.

Referee camps, which are weekend live-in clinics, offer a challenging and intensive exposure to the Laws, refereeing, and to instruction. Almost 2000 participants in eight locations learn from experienced instructors, including Ken Aston, former FIFA referee and internationally respected authority on the Laws and their application. A unique offshoot of the Aston experience is the Ken Aston Cup, an annual tournament where officiating teams compete for first, second and third place awards.

JOHN OUELLETTE
of The American Youth Soccer Organization

"If you are a positive role model for emotional control, mental toughness, trust, and ethics, we need you."

How do you tell young men they are winners when they've won 5 of 46 games? And how do you tell young women who have lost only 3 of 45 games that winning games is not their reason for playing? John Ouellette coaches both at Northridge High in Layton, Utah. He's convinced everyone, including parents, players, and administrators, that the game is a lesson in life, and the game's result is secondary. At Northridge, you win graciously and you lose graciously.

Like most high school coaches, Ouellette has another job, and it's one of the most visible and influential in the soccer world. As National Director of Coaching for AYSO, the Massachusetts native has a platform and a plan which challenges and converts thousands of volunteers to his theme. The "Kids Before the Game" approach to life governs all that he does, and he tells it over and over and over again. With a volunteer staff of 15 and administrative staff help from the AYSO Support Center, Ouellette oversees, among other things, the certification of youth, intermediate, and advanced coaches. Each course, each conversation, almost each word that leaves his desk is designed to be a consistent AYSO message: Sportsmanship and ethical behavior among coaches, referees, and parents to provide a fair, fun, and safe environment for children and youth. AYSO coaches are reminded of their privileges and responsibilities during the 65 hours (average time they will spend with their team) of coaching time.

There are few coaches who know more about refereeing than John. He's a National 1 referee, and whistles as many as 50 games a year in games and tournaments in his home region. In 20 years of coaching, he has never had a yellow or red card, and he feels that coaches, referees, and parents should constantly be reminded of what unifies them: they are the "third team" on the field.

JOHN OUELLETTE'S REMINDERS FOR REFEREES

Youth sports are about children playing a game, not about winning and losing.

We all must let young players, age 5-10 have fun in a fair, safe, and positive environment. COACHES AND REFEREES MUST DO THIS TOGETHER.

When players turn 11, we have a responsibility to teach them to be Winners. At the end of each training session and game, real winners have tried their very best, both physically and mentally. They will be Winners for life.

THE RETENTION OF REFEREES...
An AYSO Idea That Works

Many AYSO regions have seen the need to actively start a program of helping new referees get over the "first game jitters" and survive the comments from the side line. Today's sophisticated coaches and parents are no longer ignorant soccer bystanders. More than half of today's parents are former soccer players who have a better understanding of the game. This makes it hard for the new referee to overcome "mistakes" and learn from them to become a better referee. With this in mind, AYSO developed the "Observer-Friend" program.

A close study of AYSO referees reveals that there are three levels of commitment:
1. The team parent who is recruited to fill vacancies in the lower divisions. This individual has a strong commitment to the team and to the needs of the organization. (20% of referees)
2. The volunteer who takes an interest in soccer through the young player's AYSO experience. This referee will maintain an interest for four to six years, and terminates when the family member no longer plays. (60% of referees)
3. The fully-committed referee who simply does not want his experience to end, and will continue long after the family graduates beyond playing age. (20% of referees.)

AYSO's OBSERVER-FRIEND is a unique and proven method for putting a personal touch into sustaining a referee program. It is designed to build the referee's confidence and help grasp the spirit as well as the letter of the Laws quickly. John Enroth, currently National Director of Assessment on the National Referee Commission, began a "Helping Hand" idea as Regional Chief Referee in 1985 in El Toro, California. Observer-Friend is a further development of this idea. "This program is not meant to be a formal assessment experience for the new referee. It is purely and simply a mentoring program to help the new referee through the mechanics of controlling the game, understanding the intent of the Laws and having fun along with the children. Knowing they have a friend on the side line can allow them to relax and grow," notes Enroth, who is now in his 20th year in AYSO.

After officials have been recruited and trained, AYSO feels that a nurturing, helping hand will both improve the quality of refereeing and the length of service. With the system, "Mentors" work with "Trainees" before, during, and after the trainees' games.

The objective is simple: To help the new referees through the first few weeks of their AYSO refereeing experience. The mentor is a friend, first making contact with the trainee after the assignment has been made. With an eye toward praise and encouragement, the mentor tries to ensure that the refereeing experience is a positive one. The mentor's roles include that of friend, advisor, supporter, advocate, choreographer, teacher, coach, and role model*.

From the AYSO Observer-Friend Training Packet.

ACTIVITIES OF THE OBSERVER-FRIEND (Mentor)

Pre-Game

Arrives early.
Encourages referee.
Helps with pre-game, if needed.
Takes visible position on sidelines.

During Game

Keeps few notes.
Avoids record-keeping.
Offers encouragement.
Provides advice at half and quarters.
Assists in sideline control.
Appears professional.
Is conspicuous on sideline.

Postgame

Writes a few thoughts.
Encourages referee.
Answers questions.
Offers simple tips and recommendations.
Provides affirmation and encouragement.
Follows up with phone call or another friendly observation.

SUBSTITUTION

All registered players in attendance at League and AYSO playoff games, where they exist, must participate and play at least half of the game excluding overtime.

Such participation is controlled as follows:

1. Midway through the first half, and midway through the second half, the referee halts the game,* stops the watch and notes on lineup cards those players substituting. Stoppage is made when the ball is out of play, such as during a throw-in, goal-kick, corner-kick, following a goal, or before a free-kick is to be taken. Additionally, substitutions may be made at halftime and at the start of any overtime periods.
2. Respective coaches of each team may substitute any players or none during such interruptions, as long as, at game's end, all players have played at least half of the game.

A Hint For Calling Fouls

The more marginal the call, the more certain you must appear to be. Be fast, (no time for others to "second guess" you) and be clear, (everyone will know the direction of the kick).

CHARGING THE GOALKEEPER

Charging the goalkeeper shall not be permitted in the penalty-area, nor shall the goalkeeper be harassed or interfered with while attempting to put the ball into play.

SIDELINE COACHING

Sideline participation by coaches is limited to positive instruction and encouragement and is limited to two coaches from each team who must remain within an area that extends ten (10) yards on either side of the half-line. The coaches' area shall be marked by two lines perpendicular to the touch-line.

*FF recommendation: If the ball does not go out of play in one or two minutes following the mid-point in the half, the referee may stop the game when the ball is in a neutral area, and resume with a drop ball following substitutions.

REGISTRATION, DURATION, OVERTIME, SIZE OF BALL

Division	Age Player Must be Under As of July 31	Law VII Duration of The Game	Playoff Game Overtime Periods	Law II The Ball
I	19	90 min.	10 min.	No. 5 26.5-28 inch circum. 14-16 oz.
II	16	80 min.	9 min.	
III	14	70 min.		
IV	12	60 min.	8 min.	No. 4 25-26.5 inch circum. 12-14 oz.
V	10	50 min.		
VI	8	40 min.	7 min.	No. 3 23-25 inch circum. 10-12 oz.
VII	6*	40 min.		
	*but not younger than 4 yrs. 6 mo.	Half-time is up to 15 min.		

For information on AYSO's referee programs and opportunities, call 800-678-2976.

AYSO's referees are all volunteers, regardless of age.

MELISSA BROWERS

"She's a great young lady who has earned much respect from both our coaches and our referees. She's a super person and a super referee."
- Chuck Rathbun, Regional Commissioner
Region 694, American Youth Soccer Organization (AYSO)

Already, Melissa Browers has her career all planned out. She'll wait a year after graduating from Big Rapids High School (Michigan), then enroll at Michigan State University to study child development. "Kids are my life, and I would do ANYTHING for them", says the youngest AYSO Regional Referee Administrator in America. "After college, I plan to open a day care center, and continue to officiate soccer."

Though Melissa herself is sometimes hard to find, her job now is finding other people who like kids, turning them into referees and linespersons, and watching their development. Just 30 days after becoming the RRA, she was in the classroom with a certified instructor and a roomful of new recruits. Melissa, 17, is a good leader, and very, very positive.

As a referee, she was recently asked to whistle a game because a certain player was becoming "problem." The youngster, who had been watching the World Cup, thought that a sliding tackle, from the front, side, or from the rear, was the only way to gain possession of the ball. Before the game, the boy received some words of advice from Melissa, who is "stopper" on her high school team. The boy caught on. Staying on his feet, he played much better, and told a teammate who questioned Melissa's throw-in decision, "Just play. She made the call." Melissa's proudest moment was in presenting the boy with a sportsmanship award.

Watching soccer is not a part of Melissa's life. She plays it (4 years' varsity), with gymnastics teaching, bike touring, figure skating, and girls' ice hockey taking up any free time. Now, however, she's watching over the referees, and she truly is the referee's best friend. "We're recruiting for the three man system (Diagonal) here. Two referees is just too confusing, and besides, I want more to be involved. Refereeing is a great experience, and I want to share it with more people."

Melissa, just three miles from her home in Big Rapids, Michigan.
Photo by Kelly Bolen

HAVE YOU EVER OFFICIATED A PERFECT GAME?

If you feel you have, tell others about it, for some referees have been struggling for the perfect game for more than 20 years. There is always something to be learned from little mistakes: a wrong move, a wrong gesture which was ill-timed, a belated hand signal for the direction of a kick, or perhaps too long a delay for a kick-off following a goal. Some experienced top officials may make a large number of mistakes, but they are usually inconsequential to the control and outcome of the game.

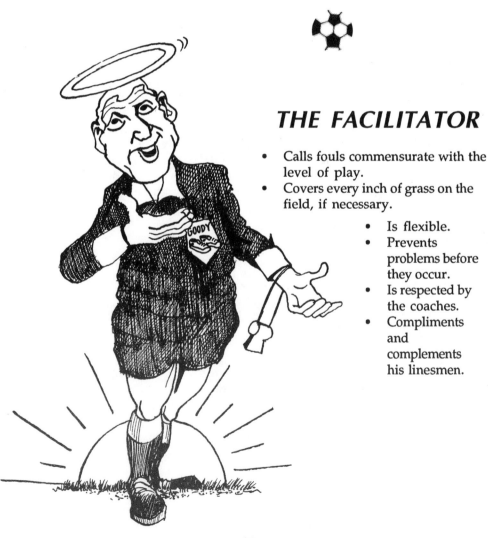

THE FACILITATOR

- Calls fouls commensurate with the level of play.
- Covers every inch of grass on the field, if necessary.
  - Is flexible.
  - Prevents problems before they occur.
  - Is respected by the coaches.
  - Compliments and complements his linesmen.

THE UNITED STATES SOCCER FEDERATION

More than 60,000 officials, from beginners to international referees, conduct games under the jurisdiction of the FIFA-affiliated United States Soccer Federation (USSF). Overseeing the National Referee Development Program within the USSF is a chairman, two representatives each from the Amateur, Youth, and Professional Divisions, and a National Director of Referee Administration, National Director of Instruction of Officials, and a National Director of Assessment. Through its various programs, the Committee is responsible for the instruction, examining, grading, and the administration of all registered and candidate referees. Serving the Committee is a full-time, paid Director of Officials. Each state Association has its own Referee Committee, with Directors of Assessment, Instruction, and Administration. There are 55 State Associations, with California, Ohio, New York, Pennsylvania and Texas each having two.

The Committee's vision is to become a pre-eminent worldwide model for referee excellence by the year 2005. Their mission is to be a service organization of integrity, dedicated to all referees. The purpose is to ensure the development of the USSF referee in terms of quality and quantity through achieving excellence in governance, education, and administration.

Hank Steinbrecher is Secretary General of the United States Soccer Federation.

USSF'S CODE OF ETHICS FOR REFEREES

1. *That I shall always maintain the utmost respect for the game of soccer.*
2. *That I will conduct myself honorably at all times and maintain the dignity of my position.*
3. *That I shall always honor a contractual obligation.*
4. *That I will endeavor to attend local meetings and clinics so as best to know the Laws of the Game and their proper interpretation.*
5. *That I will always strive to achieve maximum team work with any fellow referees and linesmen.*
6. *That I shall be loyal to my fellow referees and linesmen, and never knowingly promote criticism of them.*
7. *That I shall be in good physical condition so as to be in the right place at the right time.*
8. *That I will control the players effectively by being courteous and considerate without sacrificing firmness.*
9. *That I shall do my utmost to assist my fellow officials to better themselves and their work.*
10. *That I shall not make statements about any game except to clarify an interpretation of the Laws of the Game.*
11. *That I consider it a privilege to be a part of the United States Soccer Federation and I will strive to make my actions reflect credit upon that organization and its affiliates.*

All national competitions sponsored by USSF require the use of the Diagonal System of Control. All organizations are to strive to meet this requirement.

UNITED STATES SOCCER FEDERATION REFEREE GRADES

To provide uniform standards for soccer referees in the United States, the National Referee Committee has adopted nine referee grades. These grades supersede all grades which have previously been adopted by state associations and leagues so that uniform and comparative grading exists throughout the United States.

9 - United States Soccer Federation Associate Referee
   A. Minimum Age: None
   B. Badge: United States Soccer Federation Associate Referee, with current year.
   C. Recommended Assignment Level: Beginning referee for youth games through age 11.

8 - United States Soccer Federation Referee Class 2
   A. Minimum Age: None
   B. Badge: United States Soccer Federation Referee, with current year.
   C. Recommended Assignment Level: All youth games. Linesman in comparative games.

7 - United States Soccer Federation Referee Class 1
  A. Minimum Age: 17 years
  B. Badge: United States Soccer Federation Referee, with current year.
  C. Recommended Assignment Level: All youth games and mixed leagues, linesman in all amateur games below the top division.

6 - United States Soccer Federation State Referee Class 2
  A. Minimum Age: 18 years
  B Badge: United States Soccer Federation State Referee, with current year.
  C. Recommended Assignment Level: All youth games, all amateur games through second division and linesman in the top amateur division and amateur cup games.

5 - United States Soccer Federation State Referee Class 1
  A. Minimum Age: 19 years
  B. Badge: United States Soccer Federation State Referee, with current year.
  C. Recommended Assignment Level: All youth games and amateur games including first division and linesman in professional league and international cup games.

4 - United States Soccer Federation National Referee
  A. Minimum Age: 25 years
  B. Badge: United States Soccer Federation National Referee, with current year.
  C. Assignment Level: All games except formal FIFA international matches; linesman for international matches.

3 - United States Soccer Federation National I.P.C. Referee
  (International Panel Candidate)
  A. Minimum Age: 26 years
  B. Badge: U.S.S.F. National Referee, with current year.
  C. Assignment Level: All games except formal FIFA international matches.

2 - United States Soccer Federation International Linesman
  A. Minimum Age: 26 years
  B. Badge: FIFA Linesman with current year
  C. Assignment Level: All games.
  D. U.S. Citizenship required (U.S. Soccer Federation Rule 3039.)

1 - United States Soccer Federation International Referee
  A. Minimum Age: 26 years
  B. Badge: FIFA with current year.
  C. Assignment Level: All games.
  D. U.S. Citizenship required (U.S. Soccer Federation Rule 3039.)

The criteria for certification of referees are divided into six categories: Age, Experience, Training, Written Examination, Field Evaluation, and Physical Fitness. All referees except Associate (#9) are paid. Annual requirements include In-Service Training, a Refresher Test, and a Physical Test, depending on the level of referee grade.

Inquiries regarding the USSF's referee programs may be made to: U.S. Soccer, U.S. Soccer House, 1801-1811 South Prairie, Chicago, Illinois 60616. (312) 808-1300

THE UNITED STATES YOUTH SOCCER ASSOCIATION

YOUTH SOCCER

The United States Youth Soccer Association is the youth division of the United States Soccer Federation. The other branches of USSF are the amateur and the professional divisions. Serving players from "Under 6" to "Under 19", USYSA now registers over 2.2 million players.

U S Youth Soccer referees are recruited, trained, assigned, assessed, and organized through the offices of the 55 State Referee Administrators of USSF. U S Youth Soccer encourages 3v3 (under 6), 4v4 (under 8), and 8v8 (under 10) competitions.

Levels of play include recreational, competitive, and Olympic Development programs. U S Youth Soccer has several programs to serve and maintain referees. The "Referee Mentor" is a plan which provides a mature and experienced referee for both beginning and more advanced officials. It is based upon the willingness of officials to give of their time and knowledge, for improvement at all levels.

Young referees are actively recruited at the local level. The dedication of these referees, many of whom have played the game, is vital to the program. Among these young officials may be found ambitious youngsters who are cited for outstanding contributions. Each State Association is asked to submit the name of one boy and girl each year. U S Youth Soccer then selects a National Young Referee of the Year, for both boys and girls. The national winners are recognized at the Snickers U S Youth National Championship.

For information on the U S Youth Soccer, call 1-800-4-SOCCER.

US Youth Soccer at its best. A semi-final game at the 1995 Snickers U S Youth Soccer Championship.   *Photo by Phil Stephens*

ERICH SIMMONS
of North Reading, Massachusetts
U S Youth Soccer's REFEREE OF THE YEAR

*"My level of confidence keeps growing with every game.
The sky is my limit."*

"Life is what happens to you while you're making other plans", a wise man once said. With Erich Simmons, it was in the spring of 1989. He showed up early for his game, and someone asked him to fill the ranks for a "no show". At age 13, refereeing won him over. His life changed.

Erich is termed an "overachiever" by the local press. He is very focused. His long-term ambition, now that he has 200 games under his belt? To referee in the World Cup, of course. He gets chills just looking back to WC '94, especially when he saw America's referee, Arturo Angeles, leading the national teams of Greece and Argentina onto the field. Short term goals? To be the best referee he possibly can, and it matters little whether it's for 10 year olds or everyone's challenge, the "Under 19's", Erich knows there are hidden surprises in each game. He prepares fully, and his level of concentration serves him well. Before he leaves for each game, part of the ritual is to glance at the sign above his bed... "The Ultimate Goal."

During World Cup '94 activities, Erich was told by the selection committee of USYSA that he had been named as the male National Young Referee of the Year. He had first been selected as State Referee of the Year, and that surprised only a few. National recognition, some felt, was also inevitable. USYSA is proud of its choice.

Erich is a leader, a quality that does not go unnoticed. He's been President of his class at North Reading High School, captain of the soccer team, as well as the indoor and outdoor track teams. When asked about the challenges of refereeing, Erich centers on the positive: "I know that young referees can easily be persuaded. My games have taught me how to manage myself and others." His advice to all referees? "Be courageous, and know the Laws cold. Understand the game and what it's all about." And, an unusual caution to all referees: "Don't do too many games. You can get burned out. Have a good balance in your life. Be totally professional in all that you do." Great lessons from a winger who showed up early to his game.

HARRY RODGERS... EVERYONE'S INSPIRATION

The numbers are staggering, probably never to be challenged. For 51 years, Harry Rodgers was in charge of assignments for two referee groups, and he scheduled referees for 154,000 games. He still records details of every game he ever called, beginning in 1926. In 1941 he introduced the Dual System for college games, and in 1951 he became a FIFA referee. He is now in his 69th year of whistling. At 92, he is the senior referee in the world. Harry has seen it all.

How does he do it? Twice a day, for twenty minutes each session, he climbs on his stationery bicycle, and thinks about his next game. Mentally he reviews the philosophy that has brought him through many a situation: Refereeing takes guts, honesty, common sense, a desire for fair play, and an understanding of people. In 1988, he walked off a college field for the last time, and was 90 years old when he last called a high school game.

Most impressive in Harry's career is his remarkable record of only three "sending off" offenses, and 152 cautions. "You must have the respect of the players", Harry indicates, summing up a very full life in the game. His advice to new officials: "Get out there, and RUN, RUN, RUN. Anticipate the play, be fearless, stay in shape, and keep up with the rules."

In January of 1952, Harry sports his famous bow tie in a Sunday League. "It was not whimsical, but a statement for a referee's dignity," he still insists.

HARRY RODGERS' CAREER

Total games: 4,251		
High School: 1,817	Games Alone: 1,770	
College: 850	Dual System: 2,375	
Federation: 1,584	Diagonal: 106	

HIGH SCHOOL SOCCER

The world's game in secondary schools began on the eastern seaboard during the late 1930's. Today more than 13,000 varsity boys and girls teams play, and soccer continues its dynamic growth. Great strides are being taken to improve coaching and refereeing. The National Federation of State High Schools Association now has a national program to certify coaches. The National Intercollegiate Soccer Officials Association has become active in the training of high school referees, and has begun its first live-in camp to train these men and women. High school rules continue to move closer to FIFA Laws. All suggestions for rule changes are considered annually.

Mario Donnangelo, educator, has been active for many years in high school and college refereeing and administration. He has been Chairman of the Soccer Rules Committee for the National Federation of State High Schools Association since 1987.

XII (k)... HAVE YOU FORGOTTEN IT?

The "intelligent and gifted" player will develop talents and skills to the fullest, exploiting the opponents' weaknesses as well. The "crafty" or "smart" competitor may also be tempted to exploit the Laws for his own benefit, sometimes taking advantage of the referee.

There are players who, from the opening whistle, are on the fringes of being warned or cautioned. Some, when cautioned, know that referees are hesitant to issue a second caution. They are therefore "protected," and allowed more freedom than the player who never receives the caution.

You are expected to judge the actions of all players. This expectation must be carried one step further: You must judge when a player is deliberately and persistently infringing on the Laws. When this happens, you must invoke the most commonly forgotten aspect of LAW XII: Section k. "A player shall be cautioned and shown the yellow card if he persistently infringes the Laws of the Game."

It is your duty to stop the player who fouls as a defensive tactic, and who really has lost nothing through the foul. Stopping an opponent at all costs is a tactic which spoils the game for spectators, and may cause injury and ill-feeling. The free-kick dutifully awarded is never enough!

REMEMBER: The violations do not have to be the same. (i.e., a tripping foul or two plus a deliberate hand ball and an unfair charge by one player may be all you need to observe before cautioning. Don't you agree that a player who commits these three violations in a fairly short period of time is persistently infringing the Laws of the Game.)

HIGH SCHOOL DIFFERENCES FROM FIFA
(Numbers reflect FIFA Law numbers)

1. FIELD OF PLAY
- Penalty Kick Line (by option) - 2 feet long
- Length - 100-120 yards
- Width - 55-75 yards

2. BALL
- Hometeam provides 3 or more balls of same make.
- Balls made of leather or similar material which is weather resistant must be used.

3. PLAYERS AND SUBSTITUTIONS
- A roster must be submitted at least 5 minutes before game time.
- No limit on substitutes. They must first report to the scorer's table.
- Substitutions must be made during the following stoppages:
  Goal-kick, corner-kick (if possession), throw-in (if possession), following a goal, between periods, cautions (opponents may only substitute a like number), injury (opponents may only substitute a like number), or disqualifications, but only if for a 2nd caution or for taunting..
- Only one re-entry is allowed. Can only be done during 2nd half.
- Replacement is required for a cautioned or injured player who has been attended to on the field and for a bleeding player.
- During a penalty-kick situation, a substitute may not come on to take the kick.
- Repeated substitutions to consume time could result in an indirect free-kick.

4. PLAYER'S EQUIPMENT
- Numbers must be different, worn on the back, and be at least 6 inches in height.
- Numbers, if on the front, must be at least 4 inches high.
- Jerseys must be of contrasting colors. Hometeam changes, if necessary.
- Coach is responsible for players being properly equipped.
- No jewelry, unless medical. If medical, it must be taped down.
- Goalkeeper may wear soft billed baseball cap or headband/hair control device made of soft material.

6. REFEREE AND LINESMEN
- The dual system (Head Referee and Referee) or Diagonal System of Control (DSC) may be used.
- If DSC and referee does not appear, the senior linesman assumes the duties of Referee.
- Timekeeper notifies the nearest official audibly of a countdown of the last 10 seconds of playing time of any period.

- Pre-game instructions given re goalkeeper interference and language abuse.
- Use of tobacco products by players, coaches, or bench personnel or officials during a game is prohibited.

7. DURATION OF GAME

- Halftime is a maximum of 10 minutes unless opposing coaches and referee agrees to a different length.
- 5 minutes between regulation play and overtime.
- 2 minutes between overtime periods.
- Overtime is two 10 minute periods (by state adoption).
- Periods are 40 minutes each.
- Goal differential, by state adoption -- game is terminated whenever a team achieves a certain difference as long as half has been played.

9. BALL IN AND OUT OF PLAY

- Temporary suspension of play when one team clearly is in possession = Indirect Free Kick.
- Time is suspended for a penalty-kick, following a goal, or a caution/disqualification.
- Drop Ball nearest point outside of penalty area is OK.
- Drop Ball must be at least five yards from a boundary line.
- 2nd Whistle required to restart play after a substitution, caution, sending off, injury, encroachment, or the taking of a penalty-kick.

12. FOULS AND MISCONDUCT

- Intent is required for a penal offense.
- The act of moving the hands/arms to protect oneself and making contact with the ball is *intentional* handling if it occurs <u>after</u> the kick.
- Dangerous play if the act could cause injury to any player or self.
- A 2nd cautionable offense, or taunting, causes player disqualification, however the player may be replaced.
- Caution for any *incidental* use of profane or abusive language.

14. PENALTY-KICK

- Once the kicker begins an approach toward the ball, movement may not be interrupted.

16. GOAL-KICK

- Must be taken from within that half of the goal area nearest to where the ball left the field of play.

THE NATIONAL INTERCOLLEGIATE SOCCER OFFICIALS ASSOCIATION AND THE COLLEGE GAME

In 1963, the National Intercollegiate Soccer Officials Association (NISOA) was formed, at the request of college coaches. Beginning with 184 members in 1964, NISOA now includes almost 4000 members, and all certified NCAA, NJCAA, NCCAA and NAIA college games are refereed by its officials.

Members are eligible to receive assignments during their first year of membership. Most, however, are assigned as linespersons. As these linespersons gain experience, they soon receive games "in the middle." The average experience of new referees is three to five years, and the membership includes 18 female national referees among 200 registered women. The Diagonal System of Control, now mandatory in all NCAA games, is fully endorsed and used by NISOA members.

Today, 117 local chapters in 47 states are provided with a regular newsletter, instructional materials, national entry examination standards, an international exchange program, a complete Referee Manual, and a national training camp, as well as a Clinician and Assessor Training Programs. All NISOA officials are required to take an annual written and physical test. Another opportunity is a training camp held annually at Elizabethtown College in Pennsylvania.

In 1993, NISOA made an effort to include high school soccer officials in its membership. Approximately 220 high school referees are now registered with NISOA. With the beginning of its five year plan in 1995, it is expected to reach over 1000 members. Recreational, YMCA and church leagues have also been aided by NISOA and its 120 registered clinicians. While education, training, and recruitment remain important, NISOA also recognizes those who have contributed to the game. Sportsmanship awards, camp training awards, honor awards, and a NISOA Referee Hall of Fame Award are now part of the annual activities of NISOA.

Any referee interested in NISOA may contact a local chapter through: Dr. Ray Bernabei, 541 Woodview Drive, Longwood, Florida 32779 (407) 862-3305.

Ray Bernabei
Executive Director of NISOA

COLLEGE DIFFERENCES FROM FIFA
(Numbers reflect FIFA Law numbers)

1. FIELD OF PLAY
- Penalty Kick Line (by option) - 2 feet long
- Length - 110-120 yards
- Width - 65-80 yards
- Team benches and Timer's table - Same side of field and at least 10 feet from the touch-line.

2. BALL
- Home team provides 3 to 6 balls of same make.

3. PLAYERS AND SUBSTITUTIONS
- A roster must be submitted at least 15 minutes before game time.
- No limit on substitutes. They must first report to the scorer's table.
- Substitutions must be made during the following stoppages:
  Goal-kick, corner-kick, throw-in possession following a goal, between periods, cautions, or injury.
- Only one re-entry is allowed. Can only be done during 2nd period.
- Roster must include total number of cautions and send-offs for each player.

4. PLAYER'S EQUIPMENT
- Number must be a minimum of 4 inches high and worn on front and back.
- Home team wears white or light-colored jersey - visiting team wears dark-colored jersey

5. REFEREE AND LINESMEN
- The dual system (Head Referee and Referee) or Diagonal System of Control (DSC) may be used.
- If DSC, and referee does not appear, the senior linesman assumes the duties of Referee.
- Referee reports name of ejected player to scorekeeper prior to restart.
- Timekeeper keeps the time and notifies the nearest official audibly of a countdown of the last 10 seconds of playing time of any period.
- Forfeit if one team is not prepared to play within 15 minutes after the contracted time.
- Pre-game instructions given re: goalkeeper   interference and language abuse.

7. DURATION OF GAME
- 5 minutes between regulation play and overtime.
- 2 minutes between overtime periods.
- Overtime is two 15 minute periods (if regular season).

9. BALL IN AND OUT OF PLAY

- Temporary suspension of play when one team clearly is in possession = Indirect Free Kick.
- Time is suspended for a penalty-kick, following a goal, or a caution/disqualification. It is also suspended for a TV timeout, or when signalled by the referee to do so.
- Drop Ball nearest point outside of goal-area, inside penalty area is OK
- 2nd Whistle required for the taking of a penalty-kick.

12. FOULS AND MISCONDUCT

- The absence of a hand/arm signal by the referee does not change the nature of the kick.
- Goalkeeper must release the ball within 5 seconds.
- No penalty if committed against a teammate.
- Coaching must be verbal, directed toward one's own team, done without aids and confined to the immediate bench area. A repetition results in an IFK where the ball was.

15. THROW-IN

- A kneeling throw-in is **not** allowed.
- A handspring throw-in **is** allowed.

College-age goalkeepers in camp. A college rule states that a goalkeeper must release the ball within five seconds. On another subject, look at the goalkeeper's right foot. He has committed himself. It takes courage to call for a re-take if the penalty-kick is not made.

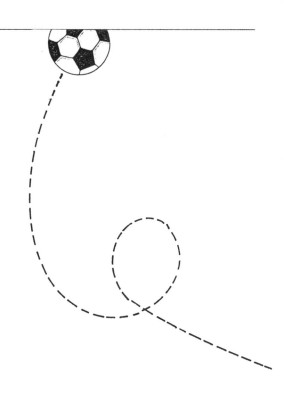

Kids have a lot of fun, but so can the referees.

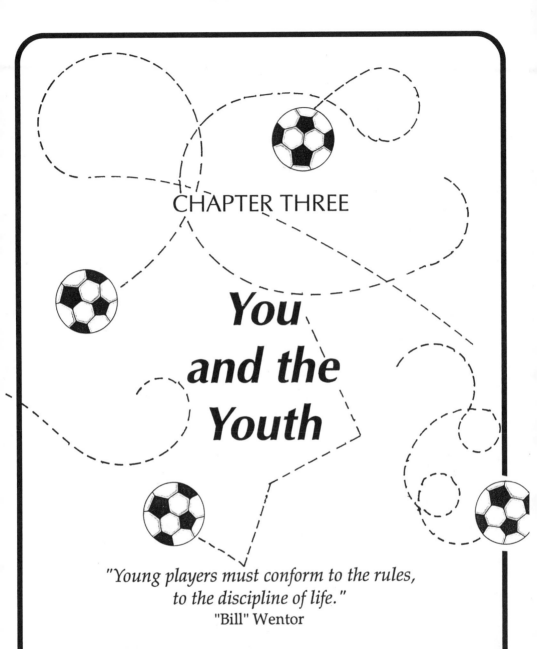

CHAPTER THREE

You and the Youth

"Young players must conform to the rules,
to the discipline of life."
"Bill" Wentor

"When I expect to be rewarded for something,
and am not, I feel awful. I feel withdrawn and solemn.
It's better to realize you do things
because they are worth doing,
not because you are going to be rewarded."
Robert Biller

WHEN YOU REFEREE YOUTH GAMES

Just as most players enjoy their first soccer experience through youth competition, referees learn by involvement in games of young players. It is here that games are most available and organizers most anxious to "fill the ranks."

At the same time, there is a great need in youth soccer for quality officiating, of a kind that will greatly increase the education and enjoyment of all. Most young players, coaches, and parents have a limited knowledge of the Laws of the Game, and the burden of instruction may fall on the referee.

THE REFEREE SHOULD ENCOURAGE PLAYERS WHENEVER POSSIBLE
Examples:

- *A player makes a mistake, and teammates react negatively. Referee: "That's all right. I once saw Pelé miss a shot like that." To the culprit: "Isn't that your teammate? He'll never get better unless you encourage him."*
- *A goalkeeper makes a good save, giving away a corner kick. There's a lull in play. Referee: (Walking by the goalkeeper), "Good save. I thought that one was going in."*
- *After a goal (the scoring team cannot hear): "That was a good goal, no one's fault."*

   The game provides many opportunities for this kind of banter. Come alive in the game, always preparing players for the inevitable decision they won't particularly like!

Referees should encourage kids, <u>and</u> each other.

THE REFEREE CAN COACH PLAYERS

Examples:

- *A youngster is playing dangerously by kicking high or "going over" the ball. Referee: "Keep your feet down and go through the ball, and you won't hurt anyone." You could even make the motions, so everyone knows you're doing your best to prevent a repetition.*

- *Before a player places the ball in the hole in the corner of the goal-area for a goal-kick, you might advise the player that the ball may be placed anywhere in the goal-area. Hint: If you suggest that the player not put it in the hole **before** it is placed, no one will ever guess what you've said, for the ball will not be moved from one place to another.*

  In most cases, the referee is to be seen and heard in his instructing, and the instructing must not be such as to give either team an unfair advantage.

A genuine, unrehearsed "bump" from a ball. Supportive words from the coach, and some "hair-holding" from a teammate. Play was re-started quickly. Never forget that you're reffing kids, and each scrape or bump is genuine.

THE REFEREE SHOULD ADMIT CERTAIN MISTAKES

Examples:

- *An off-side is called, and play is stopped. A second defensive player is seen standing on the goal line. (Don't be smug. It happens to all of us.) Referee: "Oh, no! I sure missed him over there. Thanks for pointing him out, but the whistle has already blown. We'll have a drop ball." (Note: Some referees will allow the free-kick, even though they know they are in error. This compounds the mistake.)*

- *The foul is called, but the advantage immediately materializes. Referee: (shaking head) "You had the advantage. My mistake. Take the kick, please."*

Q: Instead of kicking the ball on a free-kick, the kicker puts his toe under the ball, lifting is almost three feet in the air for a teammate to volley. Is this legal?

A: *Yes, the "lifted free kick" has been ruled to be allowed.*

FAIR OR FOUL?

FURTHER HINTS

1. Almost every injury in youth soccer is genuine and unrehearsed. Unless unusual circumstances prevail (the ball going directly into goal), stop the game immediately when each injury occurs.

2. Many of the ten penal offenses, even if committed in innocence, can be reckless or careless and should be called.

3. Pushing and dangerous play are the two most common fouls with youth players. You will see a lot of "simultaneous" pushing by two players, where neither gains an advantage. Don't call it, but give some words of advice without stopping play. Dangerous play is more serious, obviously. An experienced youth referee has said that "the only real job of the youth referee is to prevent players from hurting themselves."

   Example: Most young players, when late in approaching a rolling ball, will jump and turn their backs on the kicker (self-preservation). They may land on the opponent's legs, feet, or back (if the opponent also turns). This habit is not easily stopped by the coach. You may have better luck as a referee, by calling for dangerous play, or jumping at an opponent.

4. Youngsters become experts on very minor and inconsequential aspects of the Laws, such as throw-ins or other out of bounds situations. When you see something that should not be called, such as a player lifting the foot just <u>after</u> the throw-in, say loudly, "That throw-in is OK." Tiny criticism from players is therefore stopped before it starts. You might remember this one for all of your games.

5. Learn the names of at least five players on each team during the first five minutes of play. This will aid your concentration and may help you when you want to address a certain player. When spoken to, the player will think, "He really knows what he's doing. He even knows my name."

6. Unless some player has been placed in some physical danger, most "borderline" calls should not be made. There is nothing more disconcerting than the referee who calls "goalkeeper steps" perfectly, concentrating on trivial infractions that can result when players decide to test the referee and each other. Most children quickly forget, have little knowledge of what really is allowed, and are innocent in their enthusiasm for the game.

7. Always give the appearance of enjoying yourself. Many youth games are not particularly well-played, and you may suddenly have an urge to be elsewhere. Be seen smiling at least once each game, and try to make a poor game an acceptable experience.

   The referee of youth games who views himself as a full, firm authority with a textbook knowledge of the Laws may be missing the real joy of the official's soccer experience: that of being a consistent "facilitator" of play and of being a sensitive and sensible adult.

Q: May a player be sent off by his own captain?
A: No. Only a referee may send a player off the field.

-40-

EVERY PLAYER IS DIFFERENT

Each game is different, and dependent on the age group of the participants. Go into each contest with a full understanding of the players. Can you add to this list?

Under 8 *"Age of Innocence"*
- Obedient to all decisions of referee and coach
- Pressure from parents, most of whom are new to game
- Fear of opponent, and often the ball
- Awkwardness
- No concept whatever of off-side

Under 10 *"The Emerging Skills"*
- Openly, intensively competitive, without intention in fouls
- No dissent
- Parents become aware of fair or foul throw-ins, goalkeeper steps, and off-side
- Game moves more quickly. Less predictable than any other group. Skilled players starting to dominate play

Under 12 *"The Differences in Skills"*
- Intolerance of teammates' incompetence
- Call referee's attention to minor infractions (throw-ins, etc.)
- Will question "hand balls"
- Team cooperation emerges -- Players encourage one another.

Under 14 *"Aggressiveness Toward Opponents and Teammates"*
- Sense injustices, but don't yet know what to do about them
- Disagree openly with referee's calls
- Widespread difference in abilities
- Game control essential
- Player safety is more important

Under 16 *"Has More Experience and Dangerous Familiarity with the Laws"*
- Question authority of referee, coach and parent
- Will retaliate, openly, on intentional foul
- Great frustration with own faults
- Limited parental interest

Under 19 *"Watch Out"*
- Coach-referee understanding and cooperation essential
- Everyone thinks he or she is an expert on all aspects of the game
- Will test referees very early in match
- Retaliation common
- Obstruction (impeding an opponent's progress) very common
- Will encroach
- Much "banter" between and among players

WHAT ARE YOUNG PLAYERS REALLY LIKE?

In the famous instructional film, "The Master and His Method", Pelé is shown demonstrating his "bicycle kick". It was a mixed blessing for coaches, whose players attempted the move, usually landing on their backs with an occasional injury. Similarly, Marcelo Balboa's "near success" bicycle kick against Colombia in the '94 World Cup brought much youthful participation. Once, a youngster who saw the Pelé film said, "Pelé reminds me of me when his uniform gets so dirty."

Many kids love the mud and dirt, and that may be one reason for the popularity of rainy-day games. The referee should try to remember his own youth and to think like a young player. A referee's experience will be heightened by embracing some youthful qualities. What are some youthful qualities that you may see?

1. **Kids are playful.**   A referee once told a player, as the ball moved quickly toward the other goal... "Come on, I'll race you to the goal." The race was on.

2. **Kids are imaginative.**   A blimp went overhead and one by one the 7-year-olds stopped to watch. The referee, knowing the game would have to wait, stopped the game and commented, "Wow, I wonder if he's watching the game. Maybe he'll turn on one of his lights if someone scores a goal."

3. **Kids are honest.**   "That really hurts when such a hard kick hits you in the stomach", the referee could say.

4. **Kids are curious.**   They often seem to wonder about the referee uniform. In the above-mentioned Pelé film, some clips of the Scottish national team were shown. The team was dressed in traditional very dark blue. "Wow, look at all the referees!" was the observation of a curious player.

5. **Kids are compassionate.**   When someone is "hurt", they feel the pain.

Will the attention suddenly switch to the dog? Possibly. Be ready for anything with youngsters.

Photo by Phil Stephens

The quintessential advantage signal.
Go ahead... write your own caption for this photo...

If you are in the right place at the right time,
you will always be able to make the proper call.

The most important marking on the field is the goal-line between the uprights. The goal-line shall be marked the same width as the depth of the goal-posts.

CHAPTER FOUR

Before the Game

KNOWING THE CAPTAIN

July 4, 1994. Millions of Americans and all of Brazil wondered if Tony Meola was being cautioned for dissent. The occasion was the sending off of the Brazilian, Leonardo, following his "retaliation" elbow to Tab Ramos' head. Ramos was unconscious, on the ground, when referee Joel Quiniou stood next to Meola and showed the yellow card. "There was nothing else I could do", explained the veteran of two previous World Cups. "The man I was cautioning was on the ground, and could not see the card, so I went to the captain, Meola, and told him I was cautioning Ramos for his part in the incident. It was my duty to caution him. " (Ramos had pulled on Leonardo's shirt, and was cautioned for ungentlemanly conduct.)

STRETCHING AND OTHER INJURY PREVENTION

Basic stretching will do wonders for you prior to game time, and serve to prevent the muscle pulls that can sideline you. Don't make the mistake of young players, by jumping right into the action. Rather, two minutes or less of gentle stretching will prepare you for the rigors of sprinting, turning, and stopping. The cooler the weather, the more care you should put into your physical game preparation.

For the Groin   Groin, Hamstring, and Back   Hamstring

Hold each stretch for 20-30 seconds. Build yourself up to game pace by jogging a bit just prior to and after the stretch. Now you are ready for that 50 yard sprint to goal just after kickoff!

Other Common Injuries and Their Prevention

Ankle Sprains. Ankle sprains are usually caused by hazards on the field. Weak ankles will be weaker through ankle turns brought on by uneven surfaces. Three or four strips of medium width tape applied to each ankle is the best prevention.

Blisters. A light pair of inner socks will prevent blisters brought on by tight or loose shoes. Tape will add protection to sensitive areas. Break in new shoes and socks in training, not in the game.

Sunburn. Some referees feel is it undignified or unprofessional to wear a hat while officiating. A visor or hat is sometimes almost a necessity, but the choice is yours. Sunscreen should prevent the burn.

Heat. The tradition of the black and white uniform began in a country where heat is not a problem. The standard uniform requirement is breaking down in warm weather climates, in favor of lighter colors. Do a maximum of two games in the heat, and take some fluid replacement. Water is recommended.

Other problems include knee injuries (soft, muddy fields), back strain (brought on by hard fields and weak abdominal areas) and injuries brought on by being struck by the ball (poor reading of the game, and being too close to play). Some officials often experience the pain of shinsplints, probably from running too much on hard surfaces.

FIELD INSPECTION

The referee is evaluated the moment he enters the field of play. His trademark is *not* his whistle, but the respect he commands for the unobtrusive and silent way he moves about the field, always with full authority.

When the referee enters the field of play, his first job is to make a thorough inspection of the grounds. If field markings are poor or inadequate, this time before the game begins is to be used to correct these deficiencies. In particular, the penalty-spot should be stepped off to determine the condition of the spot and its exact location. If the spot is in a hole, it must be corrected by filling in the hole. Nets should be checked for holes or loose tie-downs, and corner and midfield flags inspected. This is to be followed by a general inspection of the field for dangerous water drains, holes, rocks, or other irregularities. If some conditions exist that cannot be corrected, a reminder of such conditions to captains and team managers is a courtesy, followed by a written report to the proper authorities.

If the referee is working a game with neutral linesmen, all of the above should be accomplished cooperatively and with a minimum of talk to players and managers. The referee must be satisfied that the field is in playable condition before calling the captains to the center of the field.

A FIELD IS PLAYABLE WHEN:
1. The field is properly marked according to Law I, with nets and corner-flags secure.
2. The referee can see both goals while standing in the center circle.
3. The ball, when dropped from the shoulder, will bounce. If wet areas exist, they should be few in number.

This is not the activity of a disciplined team. The U.S. Consumer Product Safety Division reports that in the last 20 years, 21 deaths and hundreds of injuries have resulted from goal posts that have tipped over. The average age of the victims: 10 years old.

A RITUAL... THE MEETING IN THE MIDDLE
The longer your pre-game instructions, the more you are putting down all of the referees who preceded you.

The meeting at midfield for instructions can be handled in a variety of ways, and is one of the more obvious ways of distinguishing yourself. Top officials find little need for words at this time, and by-pass this opportunity to impress team captains with their authority. One the other hand, referees who prefer to give instructions to players before the game run the following risks:

1. During the game, they may have to follow through on promises or threats.
2. Coaches can become irritated by time-consumption when players are "warming down" and will resent this intrusion.
3. Players may ask too many questions or voice concerns that need long detailed answers for clarity.
4. The referee may lose credibility when inattentive players must be silenced, or ignored.
5. Fellow officials, by having to listen and not participate, have secondary roles they don't deserve.

Two players from the famous Tahuichi team (Bolivia) loosen up before a game. Players should be allowed to warm up before a game without referee interference for equipment inspection.

It is generally agreed that the referee establishes little authority, exchanges even less worthwhile information, and impresses no one through pre-game oration.

Some experienced officials prefer to talk to teams individually by proceeding to the warm-up areas near goal. Inspection can take place, and more casual conversation can result. Players and coaches will disclose information which may help the referee: "We use the offside trap a lot." or "We take free kicks very quickly to surprise the defense near goal." This information is never shared in the other team's presence. This relaxed atmosphere releases the coming tension of the match.

Instructions are nevertheless a matter of individual preference, and there may be some situations when a few words to the captains are in order.

If you carry important information about a team or situation into a game, and it will serve you to adjust your pre-game instructions accordingly, then do so. Above all, let your whistle in the game tell the players what they need to know, at a time when they've forgotten all your words of wisdom.

HINTS

1. *Some referees prefer to identify captains through the use of armbands, or identifying adhesives, to be worn on the upper arm, just below the shoulder. Some soccer leagues may require armbands. In all other soccer games, it is an optional procedure. Some captains consider this gesture as giving the captain a special mark of distinction, which is right. If, however, the captain refuses to wear the armband, the referee should not force him to do so.*
2. *Neutral linesmen should be present during pre-game instructions, and they should be introduced to team captains.*
3. *Do not talk with one captain before the game until the opposing captain is present, for all that is said must be heard by both parties.*
4. *The use of the yellow card for cautions and the red card for "sending off" offenses is mandatory.*
5. *Very few players or club officials are well-schooled in the Laws of the Game. Do not attempt to flaunt your own knowledge in order to correct this deficiency.*
6. *All players' equipment shall be examined before the game. Equipment such as headbands may be worn if the referee feels they do not present a hazard to other players. Necklaces, casts, rings, and wrist watches are usually not permitted. Armcasts are sometimes allowed by referees (High School, Youth -- NO), if they are wrapped in heavy sponge rubber or similar material.*
7. *At the coin flip, you may be asked a question. If so, be brief and precise in your response. Do not allow players to grill you on the Laws of the Game in order to test your knowledge.*
8. *In the event of disagreement between the teams, the referee selects the game ball. It must pass his criteria for weight, size, composition, condition, and air pressure.*
9. *The coin toss shall be conducted at the conclusion of the pre-game instructions. The visiting team captain shall call the coin "heads" or "tails" while in the air, and if he wins he shall have the choice of direction or kick-off. If the coin is to be caught, the captain should be told that it will be re-tossed if it falls to the ground. This precludes any problems of the coin landing on edge in the grass. In youth games, an acceptable gesture is to have the home team captain toss the coin. If this is done, use a 50-cent piece, silver dollar or a special tossing coin, due to their heavier weights. Let it land on the ground.*

You can convey authority without being dictatorial.

THE GREENTATOR

- Sweats it out three hours before first game.
- Asks both coaches at what time they prefer to have the kick-off.
- Brings mother to the game for support.
- Carries bag of lime in car for field markings.
- Says "May I help you?" everytime someone says, "Hey ref!"
- Tells linesmen to raise the flag if they think he's made a mistake.
- Gives drop balls when there is a disagreement on his calls.
- On all free-kicks, asks goalkeeper if he's ready.
- Is seen consulting Law book during stoppages.
- Asks attackers if they would like ceremonial free-kicks.
- Says, "Play On" after each tackle.
- Mingles with crowd at halftime, carefully listening for pointers.

CHAPTER FIVE

Mechanics for Referees and Linesmen

"There is a high correlation between the accuracy of calls and good field position."
The late James Walder

"I am not conceited enough to think that the diagonal system I introduced will remain the last word, incapable of improvement.
The referee may need more aids to guard against error."
The late Sir Stanley Rous,
inventor of the Diagonal System of Control

MECHANICS FOR
THE DIAGONAL SYSTEM OF CONTROL

Although the Laws of the Game neither prescribe a system of field control nor contain specific instructions on field positioning during a game, there is a system which has received worldwide approval. FIFA states in an addendum to the Laws that "the referee shall use the diagonal system of control if his linesmen are neutral." This system makes the most effective use of the referee and two neutral linesmen, and is commonly used in club, professional, and international games. The key to efficient game control under the diagonal system is linesman cooperation (Law VI). The referee must know and respect his linesmen, and linesmen should respect and support the decisions of the referee.

Referees should not necessarily keep to one diagonal on the field of play, and must adjust their positioning according to weather, grounds conditions, linesmen experience, and difficulties from the sideline.

The following diagrams will indicate the basic system of control, followed by referee positioning at various stages of play development.

DIAGRAM 1

The imaginary, but flexible, diagonal used by the referee is the line A-B.

The opposite diagonal used by the linesmen is adjusted to the position of the referee; if the referee is near A, linesman L2 will be at a point between M and K. When the referee is at B, linesman L1 will be between E and F; this gives two officials control of the respective "danger zones", one at each side of the field.

Linesman L1 adopts the *Reds* as his side; linesman L2 adopts the *Blues*; as *Red* forwards move toward Blue goal, linesman L1 keeps in line with second last *Blue* defender so in actual practice he will rarely get into Red's half of the field. Similarly linesman L2 keeps in line with second last *Red* defender, and will rarely get into Blue's half.

At corner-kicks or penalty-kicks, the linesman in that half where the corner-kick or penalty-kick occurs, positions himself at N and the referee takes position (see Diagram 4 - corner-kick).

Some referees prefer to use the opposite diagonal, viz., from F to M. This may occur at half-time or at any other time, according to conditions. In this case, linesmen would move from their right to left.

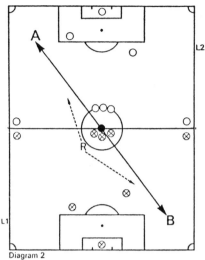

Diagram 2

DIAGRAM 2 - START OF GAME

Position of referee at Kick-off - R.
Position of linesmen - L1 and L2: in position with second last defender players - O and O.
Diagonal followed by Referee A-B.
Referee moves to diagonal along line   according   to direction of attack.
Ball -

DIAGRAM 3
DEVELOPMENT OF ATTACK
(From Diagram 2)

Ball moves out to left wing, referee (R) slightly off diagonal to be near play.
Linesman (L2) level with second last defender.
Two officials, therefore, up with play.
Linesman (L1) in position for clearance and possible counter-attack.

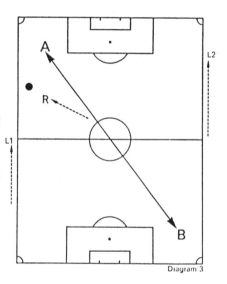

Diagram 3

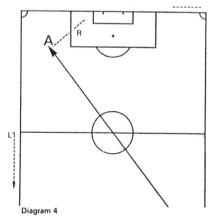

Diagram 4

DIAGRAM 4
CORNER-KICK

Positions of officials the same no matter at which corner-area the kick is taken.
Referee (R) along line shown.
Linesman (L2) - in accordance with the instructions from the referee, the linesman (L2) shall be near the corner flag or on the goal-line near the corner flag, to observe whether the ball is properly played, whether the opposing players are at proper distance (10 yards) from the ball, whether the ball is behind the goal-line, and whether incidents have happened possibly hidden from the referee.
Linesman (L1) in position for clearance and possible counter-attack.

DIAGRAM 5
THE COUNTER-ATTACK
(Following Diagram 4)

Referee (R) sprints to regain correct position on diagonal along path
(Note: The referee who is physically fit is able to do this easily.)

Linesman (L2) hurries back to his correct position on the touch-line.

Linesman (L1) level with attack and in position to see infringements and indicate decisions until referee regains his position.

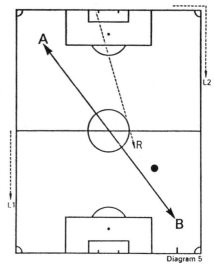

Diagram 5

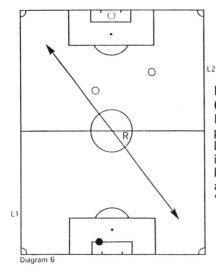

Diagram 6

DIAGRAM 6
GOAL-KICK

Referee (R) in attacking third of field* adjacent to central point of diagonal.

Linesman (L1) exercising watch over goal-kick, positioned in line with the penalty-area.

Linesman (L2) in position in line with second last defender anticipating a possible attack by side taking goal-kick.

*In case of short kick.

DIAGRAM 7
FREE-KICK NEAR GOAL
(Just outside penalty-area)

Players line up for free-kick.

Referee (R) takes up his position just off his diagonal so that he is placed accurately to judge off-side. Linesman (L2) is more advanced but can watch for off-side and fouls and also is in a good position to act as goal judge in the event of a direct shot being taken on goal.

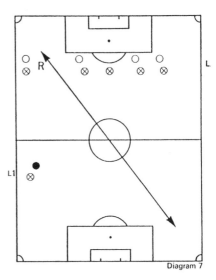

Diagram 7

REFEREE SIGNALS

The signals of the referee are for players. linesmen, and spectators. Accepted in all parts of the world, they are standardized for control and for the smooth flow of the game.

"Play On -- Advantage"

The referee indicates that an offense has occurred but that play is allowed to continue. (Don't make the mistake of using this signal when there is no foul, or you'll be using it too often.)

"Corner Kick"

This signal sometimes reaffirms the signal of the linesman. Used for corner kicks in all four corners, not only those on the referee's diagonal.

"Indirect Free Kick"

Use this signal before the kick is taken. Retain it until the ball has been touched or played by another player or passed out of play. (Notice that the whistle is not on the hand of the up-raised arm.)

"Penalty Kick"

Clear, immediate, and decisive, the signal shows the determination of the referee to "sell the call." Point directly at the penalty-mark.

"Direct Free Kick"

This signal is the first movement to be seen from the referee following the whistle for a foul. There should be no guesswork here as to the direction of the kick.

"Goal Kick"

Point early, affirming the signal of the linesman.

REFEREE

1. The referee and linesmen should discuss all matters involving mutual cooperation. The following referee instructions should be fully covered (takes about 15-20 minutes).
   a. Linesmen's duties prior to the game (field inspection, etc.)
   b. Who shall be senior linesman in case of need.
   c. The side and end of the field each linesman will take during each half of the match.
   d. The positions taken for various types of play resumption.
   e. Signals to be used.
   f. Watch synchronization.
   g. The handling of substitutions, in the absence of a fourth official.
2. Have your linesmen present, and introduce them, during pre-game instructions to the team captains.

Linesmen and the referee should be seen together, both before and after the game. Here, Roberto Wright (center) of Brazil does his paperwork with the linesmen following a youth game. His CBF (Brazil) patch says, "Arbitro Superior" and for good reason. He was highly rated for his games at the World Cup in Italy, 1990.

3. Instruct your linesmen to enter and to leave the field with you as a unit, and not as individuals.
4. Before signaling for a goal, always check with your linesman.
5. Whenever possible, face your linesman as play progresses, keeping the play between the two of you.
6. Never allow your conversations with linesmen to be overheard.
7. It is recommended that the referee change his diagonal for the second half and that linesmen change sides but not ends of the field at halftime. If the referee retains his same diagonal, the linesmen should remain on their original sides of the field.
8. As a need arises and where a special disciplinary problem may exist or be anticipated, the referee may change diagonals and/or switch his linesmen. A need may occur because of bench difficulties.

COMMUNICATION

Players communicate constantly, but unfortunately the communication between referee and linesmen is, all too often, not a part of game control. One reason for this is tradition; the flag is the signal to the referee, and there is little need to exchange other information. Also, the distance between referee and linesman is great, making the exchange difficult. Circumstances, however, do present opportunities, and officials should look for those times when it is good to "check in" with the partner.

The ball is out of play for 20 to 30 percent of the time in every game. In the 1994 World Cup, the ball was in play an average of 66 minutes for the 52 games. Throw-ins, corner-kicks, and goal-kicks and other "no-stress" times occur, a glance in the direction of the linesman or referee is recommended. The communication should not be obvious, nor should it be confused with the communication that is required for the awarding of corner-kicks, goal-kicks and throw-ins.

METHODS OF COMMUNICATION (Authors' recommendations)

Situation	Signal
Referee to Linesman	
"Time's out"	Hand over wrist
"Time's in"	Point to wrist
Time remaining (less than 5 minutes)	Fingers using black uniform as background
"Great call"	Whatever gets the point across
"I saw your flag, but am overruling"	Hand in stop position
"Give me help " (out of bounds)	Flat of hand on stomach (if neither knows, referee must make immediate decision)
Linesman to Referee "We must talk " (it's serious)	Flag parallel to ground, across waist
"Times' up" (period is over)	Cover Association patch with hand
Bench or spectator problem	Hand in stop position

LINESMAN SIGNALS

Though players occasionally look to the linesman for decisions, the signals from the linesman are for the referee. All of the signals are meant to assist the referee.

Goal-Kick
The linesman may need to first signal that the ball is out of play, if there is doubt. Then, the flag is pointed to the goal-area until the ball is properly placed.

Throw-In
Unless the referee has instructed otherwise, all throw-ins should be signalled, no matter how obvious. Note: Flag is not held across body. Hands are changed.

Corner-Kick
The linesman may need to first signal that the ball is out of play, if there is doubt. Then, the flag is to be pointed to the nearest quarter circle, at the intersection of the goal-line and touch-line.

Substitution
The flag is held in full view for the referee to see. This same signal may be used when one linesman needs to draw the attention of the referee to the other linesman.

Offside
The flag is held upright, directly in line with the place on the field where the infraction occurred.

Location of Offside
The accurate flag will indicate where the offside occurred. The offending players may appreciate this one, too.

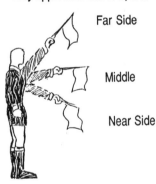

Far Side

Middle

Near Side

Fouls
The flag is to be shaken vigorously. Be sure that your position is superior to that of the referee and that the advantage has not been given. The closer the play is to the linesman, the quicker should be the signal.

LINESMEN

"I am not a Linesman. He is not a Referee. We are a team."

SIGNALS

The basic signal is to raise the flag high and directly overhead. Examples would be: off-side, a foul throw, ball out of play, a foul (including a penalty-kick), corner-kick or encroachment. The linesman stands rigidly straight, feet together, facing the field of play near where the incident occurred.

When Not Signaling
Proceed at all times with the flag straight down and unfurled at your side. The flag should always face the field. (This necessitates the changing of hands.)

OUT OF BOUNDS

If the ball is out-of-bounds and the referee has not seen your flag, hold the flag up until it is seen.

THROW-IN

A throw-in is indicated by signalling with the flag at 45 degrees above horizontal in the direction of the throw-in.

The linesman usually watches for 'foot in the field' infractions (lower half of body) and referee covers fouls originating from upper half. (Established in pre-game instructions.)

After a throw-in decision, immediately move to your location for determining off-side position.

If the ball went out-of-bounds on the referee's side of the field, and the referee looks for help, signal with a vertical flag, holding the flag in the appropriate hand to indicate direction.

Have you thought of this? Sheldon Larky of Royal Oak, Michigan has a supply of coins from various countries. After the coin flip, he gives the coin to the home captain as a souvenir.

THE OFF-SIDE

To indicate: Give the basic signal. If the referee misses the flag, maintain your position with flag raised until the defense gets either clear possession, a goal-kick, a throw-in, a counter-attack or a corner-kick.

If the off-side is whistled, stay exactly in line with the position from which the free-kick is to be taken and point with the flag to indicate the area of the infraction (near, middle, or far side of the field).

Monitoring off-side: Stay even with the second to last *defender or the ball,* whichever is closer to the goal-line. This is the universally accepted method.

Wait a fraction of a second to determine the flight of the ball before calling the off-side.

You may wish to move into the field a bit, if your visual perspective is poor.

Do not merely signal an off-side position each time it occurs. Signal only if the player gains an advantage or interferes with play or with an opponent.

DURING PLAY

Follow every long ball to the goal-line or to the goalkeeper, no matter how futile this may appear.

Linesmen may occasionally go on the touch-line 10-15 yards into the other half of the field for superior positioning on infractions.

When the ball has not completely gone over the touch-line, the linesman may indicate that the ball is still in play by a slight gesture toward the field with his free hand (palm up).

PLAY ON/ADVANTAGE (Author's recommendation)

The baseball safe sign (palm down) with the free hand is an indication of there being no foul. The advantage is indicated to the referee with the free hand gesturing in a straight-ahead direction, parallel with the touch-line, with palm up.

The advantage can operate against your game control. Do not use the advantage until you feel you have full control of the match.

PROVIDING ADDED ASSISTANCE

If a violation is *about* to occur, try to take care of it yourself, rather than placing the burden on the referee (e.g., prohibiting encroachment on all nearby corner-kicks/free-kicks and maintaining control through friendly warnings during play). Let the players know that you are there. Don't be silent.

NEVER...

- Shout at the referee.
- Leave your position on the touch-line to retrieve a ball.
- Point to your watch to indicate that time has expired. Have a prearranged signal. You could cover your referee patch with your hand (*Author's recommendation*).
- Fail to immediately join the referee at the conclusion of a period.
- Fail to support the referee on all of his decisions, even if he has overruled you.

ALWAYS...

- Attempt eye contact before making goal-line decisions.

Find the referee. In times like this, the referee needs all the help he can get.

LINESMEN'S GUIDE (DIAGONAL SYSTEM)

Occurrence	Lead Linesman	Trail Linesman
KICK-OFF	In line with the second-to-last defender.	In line with the second-to-last defender.
GOAL-KICK To indicate: Move on the touch-line so as to be in line with the edge of the goal-area	In line with the second-to-last defender.	1. In line with the edge of the goal-area for ball placement, then... 2. In line with edge of penalty-area to see that the ball leaves the area, then... 3. Quickly getting in line with the second-to-last defender prior to the adoption of a position for correctly monitoring off-side. An infraction of (1) or (2) is indicated by the basic signal.
CORNER-KICK To indicate: Move rapidly around the corner flag on the goal-line.	If a near-side corner, he checks out the placement of the ball within the quarter circle, then... • He stands behind the flag (at or very near) or • He goes ten yards in from the quarter-circle along the goal-line. If defenders attempt to encroach, call out "10 yards back" to the players. For any violation, indicate by using the basic signal.	At the halfway line in position for clearance and a counter-attack.
PENALTY-KICK If you flag for the foul, don't point direction. Move toward the corner-area.	Stands behind or very near the flag or on the goal-line at the intersection of the penalty-area line. Acts as goal judge.	At the halfway line in position for clearance and a counter-attack.

Intense concentration by a linesman in the Scottish First Division.

THE MODIFIED DIAGONAL SYSTEM OF CONTROL...
The Ultimate System for Game Control, Teamwork, and Training

Few will deny that the recent changes in the Laws have already served the game well. Positive, clean, attacking soccer has emerged in many games, replacing the "professional" foul, time-wasting, the foot-pass to the goalkeeper, and confusion over the application of the offside. Much activity that was against the "spirit" of the Laws has been swept aside.

The Diagonal System of Control, in use for more than 50 years, has met some challenges of its own. In 1973, Joseph Bonchonsky of Torrance, California, introduced an idea that was meant to share authority and to eliminate fouls "off the ball." It was felt then that "Three Referees on the Field" (TROF) would be a final statement of "presence lends conviction", and that all challenges to refereeing would be met. In 1976, Bill Mason of Palos Verdes, California, suggested a significant modification, termed "The Modified Diagonal" (MOD). Under MOD, line referees with whistles would be positioned near the touchlines, similar to linespersons under the Diagonal System of Control. The referee would still "run the diagonal", and with full authority. Line referees, running not on the touchline but slightly into the field, would whistle only if the referee was unable to view an infraction. This includes stopping play for the off-side.

Though the Laws have allowed the referee more authority and guidelines for dealing with foul play, the game has become more physically challenging for the referee. Also, tactics have improved team play and skills of players are more evident. With the modern game will come new demands for those who officiate. Today, several high school athletic administrators have authorized experimentation with three whistles. The American Youth Soccer Organization is now allowing limited, controlled experiments with three officials using whistles, in selected games of older players. As expected, many opinions have emerged. The purpose here is to introduce referees to some basics of MOD.

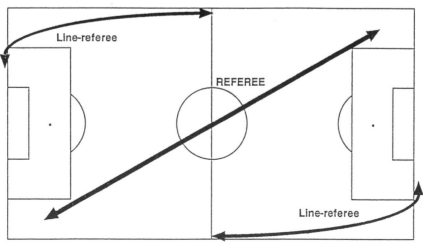

DUTIES OF LINE REFEREES

- To indicate:
    When the ball is out of play*
    Which side is entitled to a goal-kick, corner-kick, or throw-in*
    When a substitution is needed*
- To aid the referee in the control of the game*
- To recommend the cautioning or sending-off of players
- By signalling with the whistle:
    When a player is to be judged off-side.
    When an infraction has occurred out of the view of the referee, unless the advantage is to be applied.

DUTIES AND THE POWERS OF THE REFEREE

- To enforce the Laws*
- To apply the advantage*
- To keep a record of the game and to act as timekeeper*
- To have discretionary power to stop the game for any infringement, and to terminate or suspend a game*
- To caution and send off players*
- To stop the game for an injury*
- To signal recommencement of the game after all stoppages*
- To decide whether the game ball meets with the requirements of Law II

As stated in the current FIFA Laws of the Game

POSITIVE FEATURES OF MOD

- The referee's concentration will be more centered on the play near the ball.
- By moving a short distance into the field of play, active line referees will be able to view play on the "blind" side of the referee.
- Teamwork of officials will be evident, meaning more control
- Players will be able to sense authority in all areas of the field, and fewer fouls will result.
- New referees may be easier to recruit as line referees. With some experience, they can be assigned more quickly as center referees.
- The contribution of older, experienced referees can be extended.

CAUTIONARY ASPECTS OF MOD

- More obstacles on the field.
- Potentially more stoppages of play.
- Potentially greater inconsistency (3 opinions).
- Effective use of advantage may be jeopardized.
- Possible abuse of power by line referees.

THE ONE REFEREE SYSTEM...
The Multiple Diagonal?

Every referee will occasionally be faced with an unanticipated situation... there will be no linesmen available for the game. Since you will be preoccupied with other pre-game duties, it is advisable to ask each coach to locate an individual who will act in the capacity of club linesman. When you are introduced to these two individuals, present a flag to each and give your instructions.

INSTRUCTIONS TO CLUB LINESMEN

1. Raise the flag each time the ball goes over the touchline (side-line) on your side of the field. The ball must be completely over the line, either in the air or on the ground. The linesman indicates which team is to be awarded the throw-in, subject to the decision of the referee.
2. If the flag does not receive the attention of the referee, keep it raised until it is acknowledged.
3. Attempt to keep players, spectators, and coaches at least one yard back from the touch-line.
4. If there is any problem either on the touch-line or in the general spectator or coaches' area that needs the referee's attention, raise the flag overhead, keeping the shaft parallel with the ground.

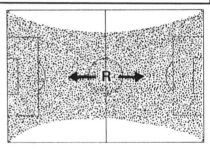

In whistling under this system, the referee must make several adjustments from the diagonal system of control. The following pattern of control is advised:

The referee (R) keeps up with play, wherever it may be. Some referees call this the "multiple diagonal" system.

SUGGESTED PRE-GAME INSTRUCTIONS TO PLAYERS

Do not stop playing just because you believe a player(s) may be off-side.

The club linesmen, one from each team, will declare all balls over the touch-line by raising the flag. All other decisions come from the referee.

HINTS:

- *CORNER KICKS.. A corner kick brings on several specific responsibilities, and your position is highly important. A location on the goal-line, about ten yards from the goal post nearer to the corner-kick, is your best position. You must be off of the field of play, just enough so that if the ball should strike you, it will already have left the field. From this position you can first monitor encroachment on the corner, making sure that players are ten yards from the kicker. You are also in good position to watch for kicks going over the goal-line, and for infractions before and during the flight of the ball. Finally, you are able to see balls over the goal-line, out of play or into the goal.*

- **PENALTY KICKS.** *Use an ounce of prevention here. Warn both teams about encorachment into the penalty-area and penalty-arc before the ball travels its circumference. This is done immediately after you have identified the kicker. Take a position where the penalty-area line meets the goal-line. This will enable you to judge all encroachment, kicker and goalkeeper violations, and to make decisions on whether or not the ball wholly crosses the goal-line between the posts and under the crossbar.*
- **THROW-INS.** *Move within 15 yards of the thrower, and slightly toward the goal where you think the throw-in will be made.*
- **FREE-KICKS In Midfield.** *After making sure the ball is properly placed, move away at least 15 yards toward the goal where you think the kick will be made.*
- **FREE-KICKS Near Goal.** *After correct ball placement and the "ten yards" requirement is met on the "ceremonial" free kick, take a position on the goal-line, about ten yards from the nearest upright. As the kick is taken, make sure you are just off the field of play, yet in position to judge a valid goal.*
- **GOAL KICKS.** *For younger players, position yourself about 18 yards from the goal-line, near the penalty-area. For older players, station yourself near the location where you think the goal-kick is most likely to be played after leaving the penalty-area.*

MORE POINTS TO REMEMBER:

You may want to use a second whistle to start play on free-kicks. This will earn you more time for positioning, particularly on free-kicks near goal.

Ease your mind by recognizing that no referee, no matter what his physical condition or game experience, can be in perfect position for all possible off-side calls. The off-side usually results from long, rather than short passes. Watch the defenders during play. Their participation in the attack or the defense will determine how many off-side positions you may have to whistle. Do they move up to attack, or drop back to defend? You will have these answers in the first few minutes of play.

Be wise in positioning your club linesmen. They are usually more effective when on the opposite side of their team's supporters and players. This minimizes their support of their team.

Whether you're on your own or with neutral linesmen, no one wants to hear which Law you'll be enforcing.

SMALL-SIDED SOCCER...
"The games within the penalty-area."

> ### "Five-A-Side will replace 11-A-Side in 25-30 years as the main football (soccer) game."
> FIFA Secretary Sepp Blatter
> Before the start of the 1992 FIFA 5-A-Side World Championship in Hong Kong

Small-sided soccer (SSS), sometimes called micro soccer, has been encouraged by many organizers and coaches as the preferred way for youngsters to begin their playing days.

Games are played on small fields, often no larger than the penalty-area of a regulation field, and play may consist of anything from 3v3 (3 versus 3) to 7v7.

According to most experts, these truncated fields and team rosters lead to more goals, greater player exposure to the ball, increased skill development, and a more positive experience for players, referees, coaches, and parents. With the ball constantly at the feet, unlimited free substitution and a simplicity that disdains many Laws that govern 11-a-side soccer, the experience is a positive move back to the environment that kids have enjoyed since the game began. Each game is like a backyard "pick-up".

Rules for play vary within communities. New soccer referees appear as receptive as most parents and players, for the following reasons:

- SSS's rules are simple, without off-side, goalkeepers, or penalty-kicks.
- The game is fast and open, with no "clutter" of players.
- The referee is always near play.
- There is little pressure on the officials. Not even the score is recorded in most leagues.
- It is the best environment for learning. Everyone gets "hooked" on soccer and its action. No one stands around.

There's plenty of action with Small-Sided Soccer.
Photo courtesy of Tony Waiters, Developer of Mini-Soccer.

THE TWO REFEREE (DUAL) SYSTEM...
An Epitaph

For fifty years, the Two Referee, or Dual System (DS), has been employed in various organizations and leagues throughout the United States. The DS thrived in places where there was an acute shortage of referees, referee recruiters, and referee training and retention programs.

With the game's growth and popularity have come more referees. They are better prepared, more qualified, and with the new changes in the Laws, better able to control games. They remain in the game longer as referees. Many also act as linesmen, so newcomers may gain experience "in the middle." These positive developments bring more officials to the field of play, and almost everyone agrees that the DS has outlived its usefulness.

If you arrive at the field and there is no referee, one linesman should become the referee, and the other a neutral linesman. You should also recruit one club linesman.

A FINAL PERSPECTIVE

The Dual System:
1. Discourages your growth. You cannot grow while being overshadowed by a partner.
2. Is intimidating to new referees.
3. Removes you from the action, and brings you too close to the bench and spectator area.
4. Removes you from accurate touch-line and goal-line calls.
5. Will not challenge you mentally or physically. It all but guarantees on-field disagreements, compromises, and hesitation to make calls in "the other half".
6. Is preferred by neither coaches, players, nor referees.

THE HESITATOR

- Afraid to ask for the game ball.
- Spends 10 minutes before the game trying to decide who should be the senior linesman.
- Reviews the Laws before each re-start.
- Stands back with hands on hips and watches play.
- Whistle goes up to her mouth but she never blows it.
- Vaguely remembers being told not to go into the penalty-area.
- Has never called a penalty-kick.
- Calls players "gentlemen" even when they are maiming one another.
- Whispers "Play On?"

Standing out above the rest. Knowing the game is one thing. Knowing the Laws is another. Knowing both? You'll stand out.

CHAPTER SIX

Knowing the Players

*"There's a big problem out there...
twenty-two players and only one ball.
Occasionally, skilled players
become very frustrated without the ball."*
Donald Bell

*"When the referee enforces Law XII, he must always give
the benefit of doubt to the player trying to be skillful."*
Alan Wade

The famous slogan of the Queens Park Soccer Club in Glasgow, Scotland. "Ludere Causa Ludendi" means "play for the sake of playing." You might want to say these three Latin words the next time you hear an unfamiliar language spoken during one of your games... known as "talking over the referee's head." When they ask what you've said you'll have an opportunity, perhaps, to change the atmosphere in your game.

There are many ways to score and many ways to defend. Some Brazilian boys are practicing a unique, but probably ineffective way of "building a wall." Notice the player on the left, possibly the designated "peek-er."

JESSICA REIFER
A Skilled All-American Talks About Skillful Players

Jessica Reifer, captain of the University of Hartford (CT) team, has never been cautioned in a game, and she admires Gary Lineker of England, the "quiet genius" who also has never been shown the yellow card. As the leader of her team, Jessica works very hard, and encourages others to do the same. "You can't go half-way on a tackle", says Jessica, who has played soccer since the age of four. "If you let up on a tackle, it could bring on an injury. A hard tackle can be fair, and referees need to know what's fair and what is reckless and foul."

JESSICA'S HALLMARKS OF SKILLFUL PLAYERS
Skillful Players Have:

- A "touch" on the ball. A referee can see this if they look closely. The player will control the ball close, and in different ways, depending on the situation.
- Vision. They see the game in a complex way, often making blind passes and finding openings when it doesn't look possible.
- Superior technical abilities. The trapping, passing, shooting, and heading skills will stand out on the field. Some skilled players may not have superior skills in all areas, however.
- An ability to escape from complex situations, such as in facing two opponents.
- An ability to see the whole field and to help teammates.

Jessica's final words of advice: "Referees should be aware of all players trying to better themselves, their teammates, and the game. These players should be protected from vicious tackles and hits that are deliberate, reckless, and dirty."

A tackle from behind. Many times skillful players tackle without leaving their feet.

Jessica with her #1 supporter, her mother, Carole.

MIKE DARGAHI
The World's Expert on "The *Dive*"

"I've seen this part of the game evolve into an art form."

For more than half of his 28 years, Mike Dargahi has had a special, yet unusual, mission in life... educating referees on some very crafty moves of skilled players, moves that can both destroy a referee's credibility and create ill-feeling.

Thousands of referees have seen Mike and the AYSO Demonstration Team. Their work was even recorded for the Royal Dutch Soccer Association (KNVB), and filmed for distribution throughout Europe.

When Mike goes to work, the mood is serious, solemn, and sobering. In this atmosphere of unbelief, Mike shows even the most attentive referee that there can be many unpunished acts on the field, as well as the super challenge for all referees, the "dive" in the penalty-area. Mike can also demonstrate with precision how the deliberate and orchestrated "hand ball", "holding", and "tripping" can go undetected. All of these moves are direct challenges to a referee's authority and game control.

In the mid-1970's, most of the professional referees in the United States were gathered in Tampa, Florida for a clinic and for final tests before the new season. It was a festive and positive time for all, but it didn't end that way. All of the referees and linesmen attended the opening game of the season that night. Late in the game a player was tripped in the penalty-area, or so it seemed. The penalty-kick was made. Just after the game the player who was tripped made the second mistake of the night, telling the press that "I took a dive, it was no penalty at all." All of the referees, not only their colleague in the middle, were chagrined by the incident. That player, of course, never received another penalty-kick all season. One referee, now a leading referee administrator in the U.S., told him, "I'll have to see blood before you ever get a free-kick from me."

WORDS OF ADVICE FROM MIKE DARGAHI

The whistle blows and a penalty-kick is awarded. Players from the defending team scream, "He took a 'dive', referee!" You are being second-guessed, and you may have made a huge mistake. Unfortunately, the "dive" has become a part of the game, and the players are becoming more adept in their abilities to use it.

The "dive" is simply an act by a player to invoke the awarding of a free-kick or penalty-kick by the referee, when all other opportunity seems lost. As a player, referee, and coach for virtually my entire life, I have seen this part of the game evolve into an art form. To avoid falling for this play, look for situations of desperation by a player with the ball. If all the alternatives seem to be exhausted and the player cannot maintain possession or release a shot, his response may be to "create" a foul. Tell-tale signs include a player's attention that moves from the ball to the defender or a crash to the ground that seems a bit too perfect, or convenient. Be prepared to hear a groan, wail, howl, or caterwaul.

The "dive" occurs most often in the penalty-area. If a player is losing control of the ball, missing the opportunity to shoot on goal, or seeing all alternatives disappear, keep an extra-close watch. You may be called upon to make a quick and decisive "no call". Oh, yes, I almost forgot. Be sure to stop play, caution the attacker for ungentlemanly conduct, and award an indirect free kick for the defending team. Everyone will get the message.

More about Mike... Mike has coached many years. Of course, he does not teach players the myriad of tricks he knows. His special genius is shared only with referees. Yes, he once used his "dive" in a game, and it meant the difference. "I'll never do it again," he promises. Mike adds: "I believe that the beauty of the game lies in the technical and tactical expertise of the players and teams; we need to eliminate ungentlemanly conduct both from the game and from the <u>minds</u> of the players.

Mike on the turf... AGAIN! When a player takes a "dive", he is playing against the referee.

SO YOU THINK YOU KNOW ALL ABOUT PLAYERS...
A True Story

"I had been refereeing for about 15 years, and thought I knew quite a bit. I encouraged all the kids in the neighborhood to play in our local league, which now included 5-year-olds. I finally 'signed up' the little girl down the street, and promised to ref her first game. Not ten minutes into play, the ball somehow escaped from the 'beehive', and came rolling at her feet. (She was the only one who was not participating in the 'ball chase'). She picked the ball up, quite intentionally, so I blew the nice loud whistle. She dropped the ball, went running to her mother, and jumped into her arms, crying almost hysterically. My loud whistle had told her she had done something very wrong. There was no consoling her. It was a very short 'career'. After 13 years of soccer inactivity, she is now playing on a college team. I have decided NOT to ref any of her games. Maybe a soft whistle, if any, would have sufficed. Now I know what they mean in those clinics when they say *'You cannot un-blow the whistle.'*"

"That Swan Dive earned you a 6.5 from the touch-line. Didn't anyone tell you that if you're going to dive, you might try the other team's penalty-area?"

SKILLFUL PLAYERS

"Protecting skillful players is the most essential task of the referee."

Allan Wade, *former Director of Coaching,*
The Football Association (England)

The innocence of very young players is well-known. Many new referees, having been exposed to Law XII only in the classroom, soon realize that the willful, deliberate foul is almost nonexistent in games involving players under 10 years of age. There may be an occasional push just to clear the way for an adventurous dribble, but the dangerous play is more common. Sometimes the youngsters go crashing about, and while it should be called, it is no more than youthful exuberance.

However, soccer for older players is anything but innocent. There is a lot going on that confounds the referee, and much of it is careless. How do you penalize "apparent attempts" to play the ball, when there is large body contact with an opponent, as well as an unsuccessful stripping of the ball?

Do you know when a player is trying to be skillful? Are you able to determine which are the skilled and which are unskilled players? The difference is most pronounced when the unskilled and skilled are both contesting for the ball. Unskilled players become desperate, and create fouls. The skillful player usually emerges with the ball, UNLESS intimidation, rough, careless and reckless play and misguided strength are allowed by the unsuspecting referee. It comes down to one thing: In each game there are players who want to appear to be playing the ball but who play the opponent as well. These intentional and careless moves must be eliminated from the game. Don't worry about identifying the nature of the foul committed. Just call it and be firm.

ALWAYS GIVE THE BENEFIT OF THE DOUBT TO THE PLAYER
WHO IS TRYING TO BE SKILLFUL.

Can you recognize the hallmarks of skill? Skillful players have:
1. The habit of playing with full knowledge of surrounding support (teammates) and danger (opponents). They play with heads up and with eyes alerted for opportunity.
2, The regular use of both feet (being "ambipedrous"), including the use of the outside of the foot. As you may have noticed, average players use only the inside of one foot. This severely limits their options.
3. An ability to tackle with either foot. Notice how few left-footed tackles you see.
4. Their bodies under control. Desperate tackles are attempts to make up for other deficiencies.
5. A disdain for unfair, rough, careless, and reckless play.
6. The ability to pass or clear a ball without settling it.

More on skillful players:

They...

      ...are unpredictable... use either foot.

      ...often will not give up the ball easily (brings on tackles).

      ...will cause frustration in the opponent.

      ...prefer the attack.. they are usually creators, not destroyers.

      ...prefer the ball on the ground.

      ...are able to avoid tackles through agility.

      ...are able to protect the ball.

      ...will not panic in close situations.

      ...will play balls to teammates behind them.

      ...rely on deception, rather than force.

Skillful players seldom leave their feet while tackling. A noted coach said that the Brazilians won the World Cup because they were the "best tacklers." Their anticipation of play would make such dangerous tackles unnecessary.

Q: A foul has been called. The referee signals with the arms and hand for the defense to retreat 10 yards. Before they retreat, the attacking team takes a quick kick, and it is intercepted just a yard from the ball's original location. Is the kick to be retaken?

A: *Unless the referee has told the team taking the kick to wait for his signal, the kick should not be retaken and play should be allowed to continue.*

REFEREEING SEEMS TO BE
THE SAME EVERYWHERE

- Referees should stay close to the play in order to be able to stop play quickly and to provide useful prompts on re-starts. Incidents with highly emotional players can be avoided when a referee is able to intervene immediately.
- Players can learn from a referee's calls when they are clearly explained. The lower the team's ability, the more verbal and demonstrative the referee needs to be.
- While a referee should not be an on-the-field coach, he can help lower-ability players to save time by giving a simple prompt when a player is not doing a re-start correctly.
- One of our goals is to allow players the opportunity to think for themselves. A well-coached team should have other teammates, not the coach, doing the prompting and instructing.
- With lower-ability teams, incidental hand balls are quite common. A referee should only call hand balls that are clearly deliberate and result in an advantage to the offending player.

Do the above directives to referees seem familiar? They are among the guidelines for referees who recently participated in the World Special Olympic Games. The Special Olympics was established in 1968 to provide mentally retarded children and adults with an Olympic-type sporting experience.

Before the US-Italy game in the 1995 Special Olympics.

NOT ALL PLAYERS ARE THE SAME...
Rob Mouw of Wheaton Christian High (ILL)
"The fans were shocked, for it was a most unusual situation. I've coached him for four years. He's an outstanding individual, and I'm not surprised."
- Wes Dusek, Coach

A coach of 22 years, talking about one of his players. Rob is the leading scorer in the school's 25 years of soccer, but there's a lot more to it than that.

Rob has been around the game a long time. He's coached kids in the summer camps, and even played for Hank Steinbrecher, General Secretary of the United States Soccer Federation. That was when Hank's team was not the U.S. National Team, but the Glen Ellyn soccer club. Rob has attracted a lot of attention in scoring 57 goals for Wheaton Christian, but nothing like the goal against Aurora Waubonsie Valley, in his last home game.

Wheaton was down 3-2, with seconds left on the stadium clock. Rob collected the ball near midfield, beat the defenders and the goalkeeper, and slotted home the tying goal. Aurora, a local powerhouse, was the favorite, and it was a victory of sorts for Wheaton. Instantly, the game's only official found himself in a predicament that seemed to have no solution. The day had been dark and rainy, and the coaches had decided that the clock (with no horn) would be official, and that it would not be stopped. Just before scoring the goal, Rob had looked up, and it registered the bad news: 00:00. But he wasn't sure who was keeping time, and hearing no whistle, he put the ball away... GOAL! Now, a bitter controversy that no one wanted.

Moments earlier, the referee had glanced toward, and misread the clock. His eyes were on the one-man attack on goal. With the ball in the net and with unhappy Aurora players surrounding him, the referee made the decision of his life: He declared the game a tie, and left the field. Back to Rob Mouw, the kid's model in summer soccer camps, and the sought-after striker headed for college. As soon as he found that the clock he had seen was official, he knew what to do. Coaches Wes Dusek and Steve Hellier were told by Rob that he saw the clock, and was sure the goal was not fair. There was no hesitation. The three of them went to the opposing coach, declaring that Aurora should be the winner, and that they did not want to win unfairly. Rob summed it up: "To have tied the game, I mean, really, who cares? Doing the right thing is more important. If you are given the opportunity to do something right, you shouldn't pass it up."

> *We have intentionally asked not to be told the official result of the Wheaton-Aurora game. We applaud Rob and his coaches for their acts of sportsmanship, fairness, and respect for their opponents. We also need to remind referees that in many cases we create our own problems.*

WHAT IS A "PAREJA"?
Knowing the game and its elements....
some guidelines for success.

"There are some people who are around soccer their whole lives, and never understand it." - *Fred Schmalz*

In most games, there are at least two players who work very well together. They form links on the field, and have a communication all of their own. They are a "pareja" (coupling), not to be separated by the defense, and are fiercely loyal to each other. Are you able to recognize this relationship on a field? How would this kind of knowledge help you in a game? If you have the chance, do you watch players in their warm-ups and are you particularly watchful in the first few minutes of the game? Are you able to anticipate the kind of game that has been placed in your care?

Even as players stretch and warm up, there is much you can learn about the team.

Even before the kickoff, you can be "into" the game, knowing what players may be likely to do. Too often, referees approach all of their games in the same manner. Be aware of the variety that exists on the field. No two players will react the same to a situation. Each skirmish for the ball, each tackle, each transition from defense to offense, from offense to defense is different, and will place special demands on you.

HOW TO ANTICIPATE WHAT MAY HAPPEN IN YOUR GAME

- Is the team disciplined in its preparation? Do players warm up and stretch, or are they just "kicking in" at goal?
- Are the players self-motivated, or is the coach leading it all?
- Are the players communicating?
- Is the team organized?
- Do they seem to have a plan? (try to be about 10 yards away when instructions are given by coaches.)
- Are players working on their roles? (long balls, short passing, throw-ins during the warm-ups)
- How do the players relate to one another? What is their level of communication? Do they appear to be helping one another?

BEGINNING YOUR TACTICAL PLAY... YOUR MENTAL CHECKLIST

Your assignment will yield better results if you are preparing for the game before the kick-off, sometimes from the moment you receive your assignment. Are you thinking about the:

- Skill level of players?
- Reputation and won and lost record of teams?
- Weather?
- Location, size, and condition of field?
- Surrounding conditions (noise, structures, adjacent fields)?
- Location of spectators and team personnel?
- Experience you bring to the game?
- Linesmen's experience?
- Experience you have with these linesmen?
- Your physical condition? (Should you REALLY have accepted this game?)

A Short-Cut to Experience: *A college referee was being assessed through the use of a tape recorder by an assessor in the stands. During the game, the assessor said that the bench area could be a problem, as it was located too close to the touchline. Late in the game, which was well-officiated, but very intense, a player picked up a ball for a throw-in immediately in the area of the opponents' bench. He got into a struggle for the ball with a substitute on the bench. The player threw a punch at the substitute, and there was an immediate brawl. The game had to be abandoned. This could probably all have been avoided with some careful pre-game inspection of the bench area, and a relocation of the bench.*

Q: A goalkeeper stands on the goal-line for the taking of a penalty-kick, after an unpopular decision. Seemingly in protest, he is standing next to the upright. Is this ungentlemanly conduct?

A: Yes, the goalkeeper should be cautioned and shown the yellow card before the referee signals for the kick to be taken.

WHEN THE GAME STARTS

Your questions that could lead to your superior performance:

- What is the attacking (and defending) method of the two teams?
- Where are the skilled players? The weak players?
- Is there an aggressive goalkeeper?
- Do the teams favor short or long passing?
- Are balls played in the air (possible fouls to the upper body), or on the ground (fouls to the lower or mid-body)?
- Is the whole field being used, or are the attacks "up the middle"?
- Is there seemingly planned play, or is it all by chance?

"Hey, what's that guy doing in our perfect wall?" Not much discipline or coaching here. It is difficult to whistle a game of undisciplined and uncoached players.

In the first two minutes of a game you will know what kind of a game you are whistling, but that is not enough. You should question yourself, and be able to answer these two basic and fundamental questions:

HOW DOES EACH TEAM LOSE THE BALL and WHAT DO THEY DO TO REGAIN POSSESSION?

How will you describe your game when it is over? If you say, "The blues dominated, 3-1, and I had no problems with player discipline", you may be missing the real soccer.

Know WHY things are happening on the field. It will increase your enjoyment and the enjoyment of players, coaches and spectators.

WHY I BECAME A REFEREE...

REASON # 112

They asked me to be a club linesperson. All I had to do was wave the flag for a ball out of bounds.

That was OK until everyone started disagreeing with me.

I thought I might as well get a uniform

It's harder to disagree with someone in a uniform!

CHAPTER SEVEN

The
Laws
Almanac

*"The referee is the custodian of the Laws,
not the writer."*
John Trino

*"The mystique of the Laws has been broken.
The fever of change has taken hold."*
Paul Gardner

A meeting of the minds for the future: Pictured left, George Cumming, Development Director (Referees and Education) for the Scottish Football Association, who oversees 2500 registered referees. George is technical advisor for the International Football Association Board.
Centered is Bill Mason, member of the USSF Referee Committee and also FIFA Law interpreter for the American Youth Soccer Organization.
At the right is Paolo Casarin who is a member of the Union of European Football Association (UEFA) Referee's Committee, and who was active in the referees' training and performance for World Cup '94.

THE INTERNATIONAL BOARD...
How The Laws of the Game Are Changed.

Recent changes in the Laws of the Game have brought much interest as to how these changes actually came about. Though there are few changes to the field of play (the penalty-arc was added in 1937), the Laws and how they are applied is greatly affecting all who participate in soccer.

The International Football Association Board (IB) meets between mid-February and mid-March of each year. The IB consists of representatives from the four British Associations and FIFA. These countries (England, Scotland, Wales and Northern Ireland) each have one vote. FIFA, representing all of its member countries, also has four. Six affirmative votes are required for a change to be accepted. Therefore, no changes in the Law may take place without the approval of FIFA.

Any country may propose a change. If the United States Soccer Federation, for instance, wanted to propose a change replacing the throw-in with a "kick-in", it would be first sent to FIFA for discussion and consideration. If FIFA considers the proposal worthy, it will be brought to the attention of the International Board.

Many changes in the Laws are the result of experiments which FIFA and the IB have first authorized. FIFA itself experimented with time-outs available to each team during each half of the FIFA Women's World Cup in June of 1995.

The United States Interregional Soccer League, based in Irving, Texas, has also received permission to experiment with several of the Laws of the Game.

Included are the following rule changes for regular season play in the USISL:

- **GOAL SIZE.** The goal size has been enlarged to 28' x 8'6" for the Southwest division, and 25'6" x 8'6" for the Southeast division.
- **MULTIPLE FOULS.** A free-kick at the top of the penalty-arc or a 35 yard shootout is awarded when multiple fouls occur.
- **PROFESSIONAL FOUL ENCROACHMENT.** Encroachment on free-kicks within 35 yards of goal brings a caution plus the ball being moved to within 15 yards of goal. A 35 yard shootout (1 on 1 with the goalkeeper) occurs if a player deliberately fouls on a goal-scoring opportunity. The player who fouled is also sent off. Players who foul five times in a game shall be sent off, with an allowed substitute. The second player on a team sent off for five fouls shall be sent off, with no substitute, and a 35 yard shootout is awarded.
- **CORNER-KICK.** An enlarged quarter circle is used. Short corners are taken from the intersection of the penalty-area and goal-line, if the ball goes out of play between the goal and the penalty-area line. Other corner-kicks are taken from the intersection of the end and side lines.
- **THROW-IN.** A ball may be thrown or kicked (indirect) in from the touch-line.
- **SHOOTOUT.** A shootout involving the "best of five", then sudden victory, will settle games at the end of overtime. All players except the shooter and the defending goalkeeper shall be at or beyond the midfield line. At the whistle signal the ball is live, with no restrictions.
- **GAME LENGTH.** Playing times is 60 minutes. Time will be stopped for all out-of-bounds and dead-ball situations except for quick restarts from fouls. Overtime is two 10 minute periods of sudden death play.

LAW I - THE FIELD OF PLAY

(All undesignated distances in yards)

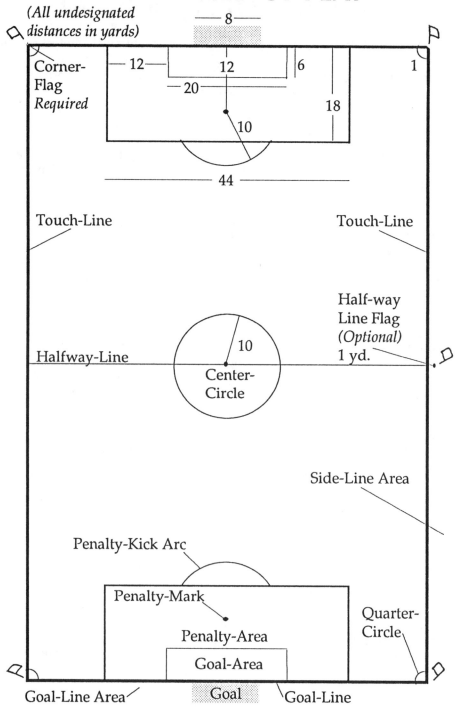

Corner-Flag *Required*

Touch-Line

Touch-Line

Half-way Line Flag *(Optional)* 1 yd.

Halfway-Line

Center-Circle

Side-Line Area

Penalty-Kick Arc

Penalty-Mark

Penalty-Area

Quarter-Circle

Goal-Area

Goal-Line Area

Goal

Goal-Line

LAW I - THE FIELD OF PLAY

AREAS

GOAL	8 Yards - Width 8 Feet- Height	• Width and height of goals are inside measurements. • Width and depth of posts and cross-bars are a maximum of 5 inches. • A rope is not a satisfactory substitute for a cross-bar when a game is played under competitive rules. • A net, if used, should extend not less than 5 feet beyond the goal-line. • Posts and bars are made of wood, metal, or other approved material. • Goalposts must be white.
GOAL- AREA	20 Yards - Wide 6 Yards - Deep	• The space within the inside areas of the field of play includes the width of the lines marking those areas.
PENALTY- AREA	44 Yards - Wide 18 Yards - Deep	
CORNER- AREA	1 Yard Radius from corner	
PENALTY- MARK	12 Yards from Goal-Line	• From front of goal-area. • Mark = 9 inch diameter spot or 6 Yards • From front of penalty-area.
CENTER- CIRCLE	10 Yard Radius	

Lines - Maximum of 5 inches in width (2 1/2 to 3 inches advised); part of the areas they limit. Goal-lines must be the same width as the goal-posts and cross-bar. Touch-lines and goal-lines are part of the field of play.

	FIFA	INTERNATIONAL MATCHES
TOUCH-LINE	100 yards minimum 130 yards maximum	110 yards 120 yards
GOAL-LINE	50 yards minimum 100 yards maximum	70 yards 80 yards

(The field of play must be rectangular)

OLYMPIC FINALS AND WORLD CUP   115 x 74 yards
Youth, Women's, and Veteran's (over 35 years) may use a smaller field and a smaller goal.

FLAGS - 5 feet high (minimum) - Blunted end.

CORNER	Required
HALFWAY-LINE	1 yard (minimum) from the touch-line at midfield. Optional

No, it's not a land-mine, but something that could be an assault on your safe conduct of the game.

An immaculate field, with two international teams in a prestigious tournament. Who forgot the corner flag? What will you do if this happens to you?

THE AGITATOR

- Tells the coach that this is the poorest field he has ever reffed on.
- Demonstrates proper throw-ins to 19-year-olds.
- Does his best to aggravate players, coaches, and fans.
- Insults goalkeeper about his gloves during the coin toss.
- When he is in the stands, yells at the officials.
- Tells linesmen at half time that it must be their first game, and that they need new uniforms.

"Sorry, but I can't start the match until you put more air in this game ball."

THE SPECTATOR

- If he had one more eye he would be a cyclops.
- Never sees the fouls that the coaches and the spectators do.
- Often can't find the field.
- Pulls the ball outside for a foul that occurred six yards within the penalty-area.
- Can't find his car in the parking lot.
- Always points in the wrong direction.
- Tells the coach that he is not properly dressed for the match.
- Books his fellow linesman by mistake.

LAW II - THE BALL

Youth			
26.5-28"	12 yrs & older	14-16 oz.	Size 5 ball
25-26.5"	8-11 yrs. old	12-14 oz.	Size 4 ball
23-25"	7 yrs. & younger	10-12 oz.	Size 3 ball

Diameter is approximately 8-3/4"

Pressure
8.5 - 15.6 p.s.i. at sea level.
Hand pressure should dent the ball's surface 1/4 to 1/2 inch.

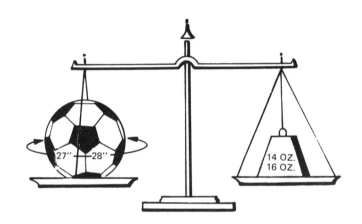

Outer Casing -- Leather or other approved material.
Color -- Not specified.

- A minimum of three balls are normally required.
- If the game is played on a neutral field, each team should supply at least two balls in good condition. Captains select one of two balls.
- The ball shall not be changed during the game unless authorized by the referee.
- Variation of weight during the game is usually not enough to consider the ball unfit because it was official at the start of the game, unless the referee considers it otherwise.
- If the ball bursts or becomes deflated during the course of a match, the game shall be stopped and restarted with a drop-ball.
- If this happens during a stoppage of the game, the game shall be restarted accordingly.

Ian Davies (Peterborough, England), was left squirming in agony and embarrassment when he placed the ball on the ground and pressed both thumbs hard on the ball to determine its air pressure and fractured his thumb. "Next time I'll kick it around," he said.

LAW III - NUMBER OF PLAYERS
PLAYERS
(A player is one who is currently participating in the game.)

Two teams, each comprised of not more than 11 nor less than 7 players (recommended by FIFA) on each team. One must be the goalkeeper.

On the bench may be the coach, trainer, one additional official of the team and up to 5 substitutes. (FIFA)

CAPTAIN
- Should be so indicated in the line-up along with a substitute captain.
- Is responsible for the discipline of teammates.
- The referee may need his assistance.
- Has no special rights.

Many leagues require that an ineligible player on the opposing team should be protested in writing before the game starts.

This youngster has never played on a girl's team. What skills and natural abilities does she probably possess? Would you treat her any differently in a game? Will the opposition treat her differently?

> "The game consists of 22 players desperately in need of rest, and a host of spectators desperately in need of exercise."

LAW III - NUMBER OF PLAYERS
SUBSTITUTIONS
(To substitute is to bring in a player from the bench or bench area.)

Substitution is:
- Done during a play stoppage.
- The referee must be informed before the change is made.
- The player being substituted for must leave the field before his replacement enters.
- Substitutes are to enter at the halfway-line.
- See "GOALKEEPER", for changing/substituting the goalkeeper.

A substitute is considered to be a player:
- When he enters the field and...
- After the player he is replacing has left the field and the substitute has then entered the field. Until the substitute enters, the player being replaced is still a player.
- A player who has been substituted for may take no further part in the game. (FIFA)
- A player who has been ordered off the field after the starting kick-off may not be substituted.
- A player who has been ordered off the field *before play begins* (i.e., the opening kick-off) may be substituted.

Number of Substitutes

FIFA = 3 of possible 5
Youth = 4 (usually)

A substitute waits to play. What may happen as the linesman moves to his right?

Of course, you can step in front of the player. Unless there is a fourth official, the control of the sideline area is a responsibility of the linesman.

Law III - Number of Players
GOALKEEPER

POSSESSION (A Definition)
- Making contact with the ball with any part of the hands/arms, and preventing the ball from movement.
- When there is goalkeeper possession, an opponent may not attempt to play the ball.

STEPS
- No more than 4 steps may be taken. Steps taken to regain balance are not to be counted. Only deliberate violations should be penalized. (Law V, IBD8). If the ball is quickly distributed, do not penalise a trifling offense. (A quick 5th or 6th step should be allowed).

A goalkeeper in full possession. The referee is right there, to make sure the goalkeeper is unimpeded as she distributes the ball.

DUAL POSSESSION
After the goalkeeper releases (clearing kick, throws or places it on the ground) the ball into play, the goalkeeper may again touch the ball with the hands after the ball has been last played by:
- An opponent from any part of the field;
- A teammate from outside the penalty-area, provided it was an involuntary deflection or misskick.

To bounce the ball or throw it up and catch it is *not* considered as being a release of the ball.

The goalkeeper may not touch the ball with the hands when it was:
- Last played by himself with the hands.
- Deliberately kicked to him by a teammate. (Trickery is not allowed. If trickery or deception is used, the teammate is cautioned and an indirect free-kick is taken from the spot of his infraction.)

DELAYING TACTICS (He only has a reasonable amount of time necessary to put the ball back into play.)
- Holds the ball too long.
- Baits an opponent by withholding the ball from play.

CHARGING (See also Charging - this chapter)

 The goalkeeper may be fairly charged.

LOCATION	HE OBSTRUCTS	HAS POSSESSION OF BALL	DOES NOT HAVE POSSESSION OF BALL
WITHIN THE GOAL AREA	/////	/////	MAY NOT BE CHARGED (IFK)
IN ALL OTHER PORTIONS OF THE PENALTY AREA	/////	/////	/////

Unintentional body contact is not to be penalized.
- Youth, - Goalkeeper may not be charged inside the penalty-area.

YOUTH

INTENTIONAL CHARGING	CAUTION AND DIRECT
UNINTENTIONAL CHARGING	IFK

This goalkeeper saved a penalty-kick. In the first 10 minutes of play, you should know how dominant the goalkeepers are going to be in the defense.

ILLNESS/INJURY

1. Stop the game if a player has been seriously injured. Restart with a drop-ball at the place where it was when play was stopped.
2. If a player other than the goalkeeper is *slightly* injured, play shall not be stopped until the ball has ceased to be in play.
3. A player who is able to reach the side-line area under his own power shall not be treated on the field.
4. No person may enter the field to help an injured player unless permission has been granted by the referee.
5. Time allowances are made for injuries.
6. If the goalkeeper is obviously injured or lost consciousness, whistle immediately to stop play. Play is resumed later with a drop-ball at the place where it was when play was stopped.

This college player is experiencing the pain and anguish of a severely broken leg. Notice the direction of the deformed left leg. Not five minutes before the unfortunate incident, which was a sliding tackle from behind, the perpetrator of the foul was observed from the sideline making late tackles and for a foul "off the ball".

The tackler was never warned or disciplined in any way, even following this tragic incident.

Can you think of tactics you might use to prevent such incidents? Instructions you might give to linesmen to assure cooperation on rough play?

ONE LOOK SAYS IT ALL...
One player thinks it's too big...
The other ten think
it's too small.

Dad: *"How did practice go today?"*
Player: *"Great. I scored a goal from mid-field, but it was a lame shot."*
Dad: *"Really. Who was in goal?"*
Player: *"Melanie. She hates to be in goal, and was trying to prove it to the coach.*

When you see this in a game, request that the player stand up. Many youth coaches divide the goal-keeping responsibilities among the team. Morale and discipline can be low when goals are scored against reluctant goalkeepers. You may have opportunities to encourage the players. Watch for opportunities immediately after a goal has been scored and during the taking of goal-kicks.

THE COMMENTATOR

- Spends 20 minutes reciting the laws to the coach before the game.
- Explains all calls.
- Tells everyone that politics keeps him from getting good assignments.
- Never gets a sore throat.
- Yells "Play On' everytime there is any type of contact.
- Takes a player under his wing and coaches him during the game.

THE DICTATOR

- Thinks it's his field. Doesn't allow the coach to walk across the field anytime before kick-off.
- Is inflexible and a sadist.
- Wears multiple referee badges.
- Tells players and coaches how lucky they are to have him.
- Makes player move the ball two feet to the left for a free-kick taken at midfield.
- Overrides all of his linesmen's calls.

LAW IV - PLAYERS' EQUIPMENT

The referee should inspect player equipment prior to the start of the game.

REQUIRED EQUIPMENT
Jersey/Shirt
- A player should not play without a jersey.
- Shirt numbers are not to be changed except when substituting or changing places with the goalkeeper. If changed -- CAUTION both players, require them to change back and award an indirect free-kick if the game was in progress.
- The referee is authorized to order jerseys changed if similarity of colors impairs the control of the game. The home team should change.

Shorts
Stockings
Shinguards
- Shinguards are to be covered completely by stockings.

Footwear
- American football shoes having a distinctive screw-in toe cleat present a danger to others, and are not allowed.
- Shoes with metal posts extending from the soles upon which a threaded stud is screwed, are also illegal.
- Players may not take part in a game without shoes. A goal counts, if scored by a player who has temporarily lost his shoe(s). No goal is allowed if a flying shoe distracted the goalkeeper.
- Any referee who is asked to examine a player's shoes should always do so.

NO ☝ ☝ YES

This goalkeeper was told by the referee that her shoes (on right foot and on ground) may be dangerous to players.

IS IT DANGEROUS?
- A player may wear glasses (at his or her own risk). It is up to the referee as to whether restraining straps are necessary.
- No metal bracelets, wrist watches or any object that may be dangerous to any other players are allowed.
- A cast is not permitted if the referee decides it is dangerous to the other players. Many youth leagues do not permit casts.

LAW V - REFEREES

1. The referee's authority commences as soon as he enters the field of play.
2. Polite queries to a referee, followed by helpful words to the player, will lead to better understandings.
3. A referee can only reverse his decision as long as the game has not been restarted.
4. The referee has no authority to declare a winner in a game he terminates. He must however, make a detailed report to the proper authority.
5. If he is late and the game is in progress, the referee should not take over the match. (*Fair or Foul* recommendation)

Look at this group... immaculate, enthusiastic, prepared for anything.

6. The referee may name a substitute linesman to replace one who did not show up, who may act until the designated linesman arrives.
7. He has discretionary powers in regard to dangerous playing. He can punish it with a CAUTION in addition to the IFK.
8. To terminate a game for bad visibility he can use the suggested minimum standard of not being able to see both goals from the center circle.
9. It is the duty of the referee to act upon the information of a *neutral* linesman with regard to incidents that do not come under the personal notice of the referee. If an immediate decision is rendered, he may penalize, as appropriate. If, however, play had continued, all he can do is CAUTION or SEND OFF. If play is stopped to caution or send-off, restart with an indirect free-kick.
10. A referee, not having seen a score, may only allow the goal if reported by a *neutral* linesman.

LAW V - REFEREES
THE ADVANTAGE CLAUSE
See Chapter on "Advantage."

The referee shall refrain from penalizing when an advantage would be gained by the offending team. - ADVANTAGE CLAUSE.

In order to justify the decision for applying the advantage clause, the advantage should be evident, clear and immediate.

Application if within:
- Defensive 1/3 of field - _Almost Never_
- Midfield - _Infrequently_
- Attacking 1/3 of field (non penalty-area) - _Most Often_
- Within the penalty-area - only if referee is almost positive that a goal will be scored.

The advantage is not to be applied prior to or during the process of putting the ball back into play, (e.g., throw-in, kick-off).

Remember, _It is a clause, not a Law._

TERMINATION/SUSPENSION OF GAME
When may the referee terminate/suspend a game?
CONTROL
- When he considers that he will not be able to exert complete vigilance over the game.
- When the field is invaded by spectators or players, and he feels that order cannot be restored.
- When a player refuses to leave the game, and play cannot be continued.

ENVIRONMENT
- If the referee cannot see both goals while standing in the center circle. (A similar recommendation for dealing with darkness, fog, rain, or other inclement weather.)
- If the field is no longer properly marked, through rain or other elements, and cannot be remarked.
- When the ground becomes so wet that the ball will not bounce.
- If a wind condition will not allow a stationary ball to remain so.
- When smog prevails to the extent that the players' health is endangered.

OTHER
- If one team has less than seven players. (If specified in the rules of competition.)
- If there are no more game balls that are acceptable to the referee.
- When the referee is incapacitated, and cannot continue, unless a neutral linesman replaces him.

If a game is terminated prematurely, the league must decide whether the game will be replayed in full or the score at the time of the stoppage will be allowed to stand.

LAW VI - LINESMEN

See Chapter on "Mechanics"

"An inexperienced Linesman can create major problems for referees. Much of this can be avoided through pre-game instructions."

Vincent Mauro, Director of Officials, USSF

A limesman finally gets it right.

- The pre-game discussion should be formal. Some referees (and linesmen) carry "reminder cards" with instructions. If the referee does not cover all situations, the linesman should ask.
- Each time the linesman raises the flag, a statement is being made to the referee.
- If in doubt on any situation, do NOT flag.
- Linesman must determine the position, participation, and activity of players.
- At half-time the linesmen should be able to help in predicting second-half tactics (from bench instructions to players).

Q: A trainer was allowed onto the field to attend to an injured player. He left his small bag on the field and it wasn't noticed until the attack proceeded against the trainer's team. There was a breakaway but the ball glanced off the bag, not changing direction. The referee allowed the resulting goal. Was he right?

A: *If, in the opinion of the referee, the incident had insignificant effect on the game, he was correct in allowing the goal.*

LAW VII - DURATION OF GAME

At the start of each half or overtime period, playing time begins from the moment the ball is legally put into play (travels its circumference in a forward direction), not on the sounding of the whistle. There is a running clock, and time is stopped only at the referee's discretion. Linesmen should keep "backup time".

TIME ALLOWANCE
- Treatment of injuries when a player cannot be safely removed from the field.
- Lost (or not easily recovered) ball or one in need of replacement.
- Time wasting by either team.
- Extension of time for penalty-kick.
- Substitution.
- Player kicking, throwing, or carrying the ball away after referee has stopped play.
- Player standing in front of ball, preventing a free-kick from being taken.
- Player intentionally taking a free-kick from a wrong position in an attempt to force the referee to require a retake.

If, at the end of a period, an error in timing (shortage) is noted, and called to the referee's attention by a neutral linesman and acknowledged, the players must be called back onto the field and play must continue for the duration of the shortage.

Time losses occurring in one period may not be added to another.

The duration of the game may not be protested.

Game Time

FIFA	Youth
Two Equal Periods of 45 minutes	Two Equal Periods of: Under 19 - 45 minutes Under 16 - 40 minutes Under 14 - 35 minutes Under 12 - 30 minutes Under 10 - 25 minutes Under 8 - 20 minutes

Halftime

FIFA	Youth
15 minutes	Minimum - 5 minutes Maximum - 10 minutes

The duration of the halftime may be altered only with the referee's permission.

If Necessary to Establish a Winner (Overtime)

FIFA	Youth
Two periods of 15 minutes each. (Generally accepted) 5 minutes between regulation period and overtime is recommended.	Two Equal Periods of: Under 19 - 10 minutes Under 16 - 9 minutes Under 14 - 9 minutes Under 12 - 8 minutes Under 10 - 8 minutes Under 8 - 7 minutes

LAW VIII - THE START OF PLAY
KICK-OFF

KICK-OFF

WHEN TAKEN	• To start the game. • To re-start after half-time. • After a team scores a goal. • To start overtime periods.	
WHERE TAKEN	Center of the field	If each player is not in his own half of the field - RETAKE. The half-way line belongs to each half. Players may have one or both feet on this line.
DISTANCE AWAY	Opponents = 10 Yards	
IN-PLAY	CIRCUMFERENCE and into opponents' half of field.	• If the ball travels along the center-line and completely crosses the touch-line, RETAKE because ball must be kicked forward. • If any player touches the ball before it is in play -- RETAKE
PLAYS BALL TWICE IN SUCCESSION	Indirect Free-Kick	• If played second time before moving its circumference -- RETAKE. • If played second time by the same player after moving its circumference.
SCORE DIRECTLY?	NO	• Opponents goal - GOAL-KICK • Own goal - RETAKE - Not in play

The home team captain normally flips the coin. The captain of the visiting team calls the toss. The winner of the coin toss has the choice of kick-off or end of field. If end is chosen, the other team must kick-off. After the captain winning the flip has made a decision, he may not change his mind.

At half-time, ends are changed and the opposite team kicks-off. Note that this kick-off is in the same direction as it was to begin the game.

If there is overtime, a coin toss will again be conducted.

Note: At higher levels the referee tosses the coin. At youth levels one captain tosses the coin. In this way, captains from both teams are involved.

LAW VIII - THE START OF PLAY

DROP BALL

HOW TAKEN?	Dropped, not thrown	
WHERE TAKEN?	Where ball was when play was stopped	If in goal area - drop on goal area line which runs parallel to goal line at the point nearest to where the ball was when play was stopped.
IN-PLAY	When touches the ground.	• If goes over goal/touch-line before touched by any player - RETAKE. • If played before touches ground... WARN and RETAKE
DISTANCE AWAY	No prescribed distance that players must be away from the ball.	• Players may not interfere with the dropping of the ball.

If, during a DROP-BALL, but before the ball is actually dropped, a foul is committed, the referee may CAUTION or SEND OFF, but may not award a free-kick because the ball was not in play.
If disciplinary action is taken, play is still restarted with a drop-ball.

If you arrive at your assignment and this is what you see, you may be a bit too anxious to start play.

LAW VIII - THE START OF PLAY
DROP BALL

- When the ball bursts or becomes deflated while the ball is in play during the course of a match. (If the ball bursts or becomes deflated during a stoppage, the game is started accordingly. If the ball bursts on the cross-bar when taking a penalty-kick = DROP-BALL.)
- If the referee mistakenly whistles.
- If the referee prematurely whistles for a goal.
- The instant the referee notices an irregularity of the goal, such as a faulty or broken goal, if done prior to the ball going into the goal (other than goalkeeper moving the cross-bar).

THE DROP BALL
- It is often advisable to quickly say "Drop-ball," and to drop it immediately. Although the Laws do not require that a player from each team is present, it is customary and fair.
- The player who first plays the ball may continue to play it without it having to be played by a second player.
- When you have neutral linesmen, always face one of your linesmen when dropping the ball.
- A goalkeeper within his own penalty area may pick up a drop-ball directly after it hits the ground, for the ball is in play.
- When the ball is to be dropped within the penalty-area, be sure that a defender is present.
- To give a drop-ball when two players simultaneously kick the ball out of bounds tends to indicate referee indecision. Most experienced referees will award the throw-in or the goal-kick to the defensive team should this situation occur. If a drop-ball is given, it should be done at the point it left the field of play, as long as it is not within the goal area. (See "Where Taken")

WHEN TAKEN...
- Temporary suspension not covered elsewhere in soccer laws.
- Illegal field entry by a substitute while ball is in play.
- Ball out of bounds -- referee unable to identify the team who last played it.
- Ball out of bounds after simultaneously coming off of 2 opponents. (A rarity.)
- Player(s) accidentally falls on ball and play is stopped before it becomes dangerous.
- After stoppage for illness or injury.
- Ball hits an upright or crossbar, breaking it, and the ball remains in play.
- Ball strikes an outside agent or the outside agent causes interference on the field.
- Simultaneous fouls of the same gravity. (This is a rarity.)

LAW VIII - THE START OF PLAY
OUTSIDE AGENT

If a spectator, substitute, animal, reserve-ball, or any other object enters the field of play, the referee, if necessary, will stop play and will later restart play with a DROP-BALL.

A limb of a tree would be considered an outside agent if it overhung into the field and was touched by a ball that was in play.

The bodies of the referees and linesmen are **not** considered outside agents. They are neutral objects and are considered part of the field if they are within the field of play.

A goal may not be awarded if the ball has been prevented by some outside agent from passing over the goal-line, or if the agent touched the ball.

Following a restart, if the ball is in play and touches an outside agent prior to any other player having touched it...

- If a penalty-kick -- RETAKE
- All other situations -- DROP BALL (Kick-off, goal-kick, corner-kick, etc.)

Players that have been sent off are considered to be outside agents.

The dreaded, but sometimes adorable, outside agent invades the field. When would you stop play? How would you restart play?

LAW IX - BALL IN AND OUT OF PLAY

It is the position of the ball that is important, not the position of the player.

Ball in Play	After...
KICK-OFF	Circumference and into opponents' half of the field.
GOAL-KICK	Clears (completely leaves) the penalty-area.
THROW-IN	Has been released and enters the field of play (touches or passes the outside edge of the touch-line).
CORNER-KICK	Circumference.
FREE-KICK	Circumference.
FREE-KICK (taken inside own penalty-area)	Circumference and clears the penalty-area.
PENALTY-KICK	Circumference and forward.
DROP-BALL	Touches ground.
Ball Out of Play	
Wholly crosses the touch or goal-line (ground or air).	If the ball completely crosses the boundary lines in the air, but, because of the wind, or other reason, returns to the field of play, it shall be considered out of bounds.
When game has been stopped by the referee.	Temporary suspension not covered elsewhere in soccer laws - restart play by dropping the ball.

Ball is in play at all other times including:
- If it rebounds from a goal-post, cross bar, or corner flag into the field of play.
- If it rebounds off of a referee or linesman who is in the field of play.
- An infringement of the Laws prior to the sounding of the whistle.

Q: What referee errors should warrant the replay of a game?
A:Technical errors are subject to protest, whereas perceived judgment errors are not. Whether or not the error is sufficient to merit a replay must be determined by the authority governing that competition. If the error is felt to have had little or no impact on the ultimate outcome of the game, the protest should be denied. In many youth leagues, protests are not allowed, regardless of the nature of the error.

Before the kick-off, you might want to take one last look for problems in the field. Here's a 5" pipe, 6" deep, just waiting for someone to step into it.

Two mistakes here. The players are too close together, and the ball is being dropped above waist-height. When you drop the ball, first look behind you, so you will be able to step back without colliding with a player.

When play is started and throughout the game, all players should have their shirts tucked in.

LAW X - METHOD OF SCORING

A goal is scored when the *whole* of the ball has completely passed over the back edge of the goal-line between the goal-posts and under the cross-bar.

A goal scored immediately after an infraction is noticed by the referee does not count (unless he has applied the Advantage clause.)

If the goalkeeper is obviously injured or unconscious, the game should be stopped at once. After the goalkeeper has recovered or has been replaced, resume play with a DROP-BALL.

A referee having not seen a score may allow the goal only if substantiated by a neutral linesman.

Advantage

If a 'hand ball' by a defensive player goes into his own goal, the score shall count. (An application of the Advantage Clause)

Early Whistle

If the referee blows the whistle prematurely and the goalkeeper managed to stop the ball or if the ball enters the goal, a DROP-BALL must be given where the ball was when the referee whistled unless the ball was in the goal-area, in which case it will be dropped at the nearest point on the "6 yard" line.

Outside Agent

A goal cannot be awarded in any case if the ball has been prevented by some outside agent from passing over the goal-line or if it crosses the goal-line after having contacted an outside agent.

Field Entry/Exit Without Permission

- Unauthorized entry
  - If score in own goal = GOAL and CAUTION
  - If score in opponents' goal = NO GOAL, CAUTION, resume play with a goal-kick.
- 12th participant (actually a substitute) entry was followed by the scoring of a goal...
  - *If play has not been resumed* -- NO GOAL. Resume play with a goal-kick.
  - *If play has been resumed* -- GOAL stands. Resume play with a Drop Ball from where the ball was when play was stopped.

Q: A player miskicks and the ball unexpectedly strikes the referee, knocking him unconscious. The ball is being played in the penalty area, and just before an attacker kicks the ball into goal, a defender grabs the referee's whistle and blows it to stop play. The linesman later said in his report that he had taken a whistle from his own pocket, but had allowed play to go on, allowing what he termed "advantage." What is the correct decision:

A: *The goal should be allowed; the defender should be cautioned and shown a yellow card for ungentlemanly conduct.*

BALL IN/OUT OF PLAY
The most controversial goal in World Cup history.

An historic photo (below), just 90 minutes before the 1966 World Cup Final. Gottfried Dienst (center) of Switzerland and Toffik Bakhramov from the Soviet Union before the England-Germany classic. Three hours later, Dienst, the referee, and Bakhramov, the linesman, were at the center of a soccer dispute that has never diminished.

In overtime, an England shot hit the under side of the crossbar, with the ball apparently striking on or near the goal-line. The ball rebounded high and into the field of play. No immediate decision was apparently made, though linesman Bakhramov was seen shaking his head... "No goal."

Abandoning any interest in play, the English players pointed to the linesman, pressuring Dienst to approach the touch-line and his beleaguered linesman. Bakhramov, under more pressure than any linesman in the history of soccer, nodded his head in agreement, and Wembley Stadium erupted in celebration. It proved to be the winning goal.

In July of 1995, a group of computer experts at Oxford University presented new video analysis techniques which show conclusively that Geoff Hurst's winning goal bounced straight down and never entirely crossed the goal-line. Rational English supporters are now convinced that the "goal" should not have been.

Q: A goalkeeper is whistled for handling a ball that is deliberately kicked by a teammate to him. Instead of placing the ball on the goal area line that is parallel to the goal line, the ball is placed where the infraction took place, within the goal area. A goal is scored from an indirect free kick. Is the referee's mistake significant enough for a protest? It was, naturally, the winning goal, in a December '92 game between Bordeaux and Toulouse in the French First Division. The protest was upheld, and the game replayed. Was this a correct decision?
A: Yes.

LAW XI - OFF-SIDE

A player is in an off-side position if he is nearer the opponents' goal-line than THE BALL. (See diagram 1=D1) at the moment the ball is played by a teammate (D3).

The off-side is called if the player is in an off-side position* and he is involved in active play by:
- Interfering with play or,
- Interfering with an opponent, or
- Gaining an advantage by being in that position.

Not in Off-side Position (exceptions)

Two opponents are nearer their goal-line than he is. (D2) (D3)	Being in line, level with an opponent, is not being nearer to the goal-line. (D5)
He is in his own half of the field of play. (D11)	A player with both feet on the halfway line is still in his own half of the field.

Not Off-side, even if in Off-side Position

Receives the ball directly from a...	• This protection ends when another player plays the ball.
GOAL-KICK CORNER-KICK (D8) THROW-IN (D7)	• A player in an off-side position should be penalized for being off-side if the ball is played directly to or toward him from a free-kick.

*Most experts agree that if a player's hand, head, or foot is ahead of the second-to-last defender, there is no off-side position. Instead, the position of the torso is the determining factor.

Once, the most famous soccer field in America. Under the stands (arrow) at the University of Chicago, a top-secret project yielded the first nuclear reaction. This effort has changed world history. Today, a sculpture titled "Nuclear Energy" marks the location.

OFF-SIDE (Cont.)

RULE OF THUMB	**It is not an offense to be in an off-side position.** If the player in the off-side position has no chance of reaching the ball before anyone else, then he is not to be penalized for off-side.

Moment of Judgement

The moment of judgement is the moment the ball is played. Participation (for which you penalize) is judged until the next time the ball is played.

Interferes with the play or with an opponent.	To distract is to interfere
	• Standing in front of the goalkeeper may affect his line of vision and concentration.
	• A close-by attacker may be taking advantage of his position if the goalkeeper has to allow for his presence. *Authors' suggestions:*
	  - It could be considered goalkeeper distraction if the opponent is inside the goal area, unless the attacker is moving quickly away from play.
	  - It shouldn't be considered goalkeeper distraction if the opponent is outside the penalty area.

HINTS

- *A player is not off-side if he is in line either with the ball or with the second to last defender or the last two defenders. (The goalkeeper counts as a defender).*
- *A player who is in an off-side position at the moment the ball was played does not "erase" the off-side position by running back into an onside position*
- *Be aware of a team's employment of the 'off-side trap.' (Defenses move up in unison before the ball is played in order to put an attacker in an off-side position.) This is a legal tactic. It is also called the "Hungarian Off-side."*
- *A player may step off the field in order to avoid an off-side call. However, a player may not step off the field in order to cause an off-side. Caution, ungentlemanly conduct.*
- *If a player's momentum carries him into the goal itself , he may remain there without being penalized as long as he does not distract the goalkeeper.*
- *The player is not off-side if the ball was last played by himself (e.g., player with the ball falls and ball goes behind him. He may get back up, go back and retrieve the ball).*
- *When a defensive wall is formed on the goal-line and an attacking player is part of that wall, the attacking player is not in an off-side position the moment the ball is played.*

DIAGRAMS ILLUSTRATING OFF-SIDE

1. RELATIONSHIP TO THE BALL

A passes the ball. After the pass, **B** runs from position **1** to position **2** and scores. Though there were not two opponents between **B** and the goal-line, **B** was not in an off-side position when **A** passed the ball since he was not ahead of the ball.

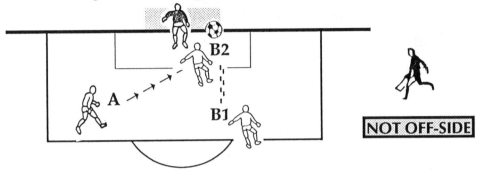

2. OFF-SIDE PASS

A passes to **B**, who is ahead of the ball at the moment it is played by teammate **A**. There are not two opponents closer than he is to the goal-line when the ball was passed, and he gained an advantage from his off-side position.

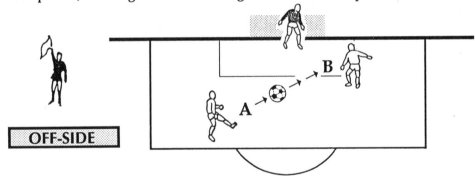

3. MOMENT OF PASS

A passes the ball. **B** then runs from position **B1** to **B2**. At the moment of the pass, **B** was not nearer to the opponents' goal-line than at least two of his opponents.

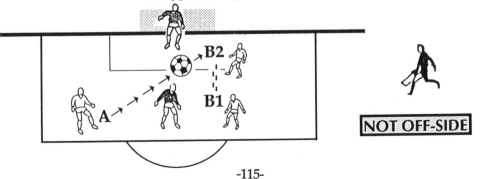

4. MAY NOT GET BACK ON-SIDE

A passes to **B** who is in an off-side position, because he is nearer to the opponents' goal-line than the ball when it had been played and there are fewer than two opponents even with or ahead of him. **B** moves back from **B1** to **B2. B** is penalised for being off-side because he gained an advantage by being in the off-side position.

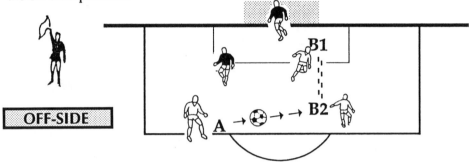

OFF-SIDE

5. BEING IN LINE (LEVEL) WITH A DEFENDER

A passes the ball to **B**, who is "in line" with his opponent. **B** is not nearer to his opponents' goal-line than at least two of his opponents at the moment the ball was played.

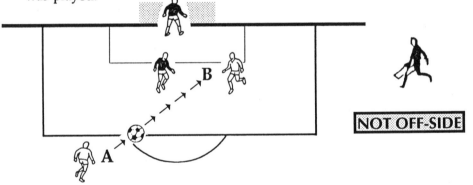

NOT OFF-SIDE

6. BEING IN LINE WITH THE BALL

A passes the ball. **B** then runs from position 1 to position 2. **B** is not nearer to his opponents' goal-line than the ball at the moment the ball was played.

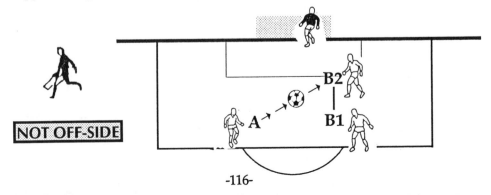

NOT OFF-SIDE

7. **INTERFERING WITH AN OPPONENT**
   A takes a shot at goal. B is standing in front of the goalkeeper. B, who is in an off-side position, is involved in active play and is interfering with an opponent.

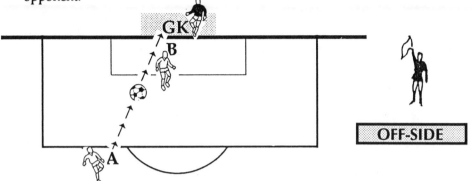

8. **NOT INTERFERING WITH AN OPPONENT**
   A takes a shot at goal. Although B is in an off-side position, he is not involved in active play.

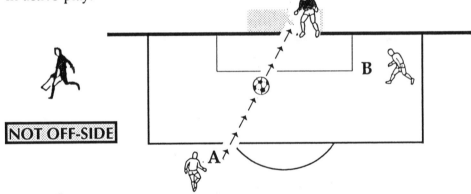

9. **SHOT REBOUNDING FROM GOALKEEPER**
   A shoots the ball at goal and the ball rebounds from the goalkeeper to B. At the moment the ball was last played, A was involved in active play and gained an advantage from that position.

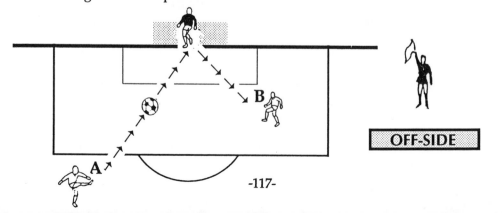

THE OFF-SIDE...
From the Antiseptic Page to the Kaleidoscopic Field

The static, unmoving and lifeless off-side as depicted on paper is no substitute for the dynamically moving and changing off-side on the field. While you are encouraged to study the off-side diagrams in the FIFA Laws of the Game, realize that they are only a "word picture" of situations that appear and disappear in an instant, as with a kaleidoscope. These diagrams do not divulge the intention, skill, intelligence, or physical capabilities of either attacker or defender. Just as no two fouls are alike, so it is with the off-side. In order to correctly call the off-side, you must know what's happening in your game.

Consider once more the new wording: "A player shall only be penalised for being in an off-side position, if, at the moment the ball touches, or is played by, one of his team, he is, in the opinion of the referee, involved in active play by

1. Interfering with play,
2. Interfering with an opponent, or
3. Gaining an advantage by being in that position."

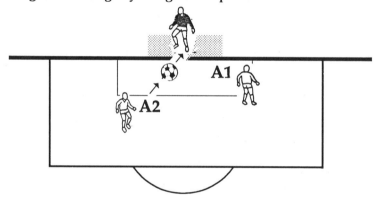

In the example, there is no correct or incorrect answer to the question: "Is A1 to be penalised for the off-side position?" Before you settle on a response, preparing to defend your answer, consider the following:

Was "A-1" running towards or away from goal? In which direction was he facing? What is the reaction of the other players to his presence? Has he been lurking around goal, looking for a "garbage" goal? Did the defenders "pull out" (off-side trap) to create his off-side position? What was his position just prior to the goal-scoring kick? Is he slightly injured, waiting for a substitution? Is he, while being injured, being kept in the game in spite of a leg injury? Is he looking toward the ground, having been "blinded" by the sun? Is he standing up on hard ground, or recovering from a slip in the mud? Did A1 and A2 arrive at their position by dribbling the ball and outmaneuvering the defense? What has been the goalkeeper's reaction to players in the goal-area? Is the goalkeeper retreating to the goal-line, or leaving it to cut down on the angle?

Don't join the never-ending arguments about off-side. Read the game, make the call, and move on.

LAW XII - FOULS AND MISCONDUCT

According to the 1995 rewriting of Law XII, a trip, push, kick, or charge must be either careless, reckless, or involving disproportionate force to be a foul. It was intended that this rewording would not change the way the game is currently being officiated. The question the referee must ask is: "Is it fair?" If not, it is foul, and must be whistled. A direct free-kick or penalty-kick must then be awarded.

1. An offense or attempted offense is considered to be **committed at the place where the player concerned initiated the action.**
2. A non-deliberate hand ball or a trip, push, kick, or charge that is not careless, reckless or done with disproportionate force ("The Big 3") -- are not infringements. Sometimes seemingly violent play is not penalized as a penal offense because none of "The Big 3" exist. This frequently is due to the players not knowing how to play the game, often resulting in dangerous play.
3. An offense normally punishable by a free-kick or a penalty-kick, if committed while play is suspended, can result only in a warning, caution or ejection (sending off).
4. Substitutes cannot commit fouls. They may be cautioned or sent off. If play is stopped to sanction the substitute, play is restarted with a drop-ball.
5. An offense occurring outside a referee's field of vision can be brought to the attention of the referee by a linesman.
6. If two players are **outside the boundary** of the field of play and one commits violent conduct upon the other, stop the game, caution or send off, and resume with drop-ball.
7. Players, when fouled, should not retaliate. Often it is the retaliation that is seen by the referee and/or linesmen.
8. If two infractions of a different nature are committed at the same time, the referee shall punish the more serious offense.
9. Two players on the same team simultaneously commit offenses having equal status against members of the opposite team. Award the opposition that which gives the opposing team the greater advantage.
10. Careless or reckless fouls are left up to the referee's discretion as to whether he administers a caution.
11. The captain is responsible for the conduct of his team. (See Players -- this chapter.)
12. Caution or send off for any foul that is committed:
    - Off the ball.
    - With malice aforethought.
    - By going over the ball.
13. Never 'pull' the ball out of the penalty-area if you are convinced that the foul occurred inside the penalty-area.

THE DELIBERATE FOUL

A deliberate foul is one intentionally committed with careful and thorough consideration against an opponent. It is characterized by **awareness of the consequences.**

The deliberate foul should be penalized at least with a caution, and quite often by sending the offender off.

A hand ball, the only penal offense that is committed not involving an opponent, must be deliberate in order to be penalised.

WARNINGS OR "SOFT CAUTIONS"

Warn the first time a...

• *Kick-off* is intentionally not played into opponents' half of the field or is subject to encroachment. RETAKE

• *Corner-Kick* has encroachment. RETAKE or ADVANTAGE CLAUSE

• *Goal-Kick* or *Free-Kick (within own penalty-area)* intentionally not kicked beyond penalty-area or an opposing player encroaches, or any player touches or plays the ball within the penalty-area after the first player kicks the ball. RETAKE

• *Drop-Ball* is touched or played before hitting the ground. RETAKE

Believe it or not, the result of this minor scuffle was a caution for each.

DIRECT FREE-KICK (DFK) -- Ball must be in play

After having committed a penal offense:

A goal may be scored "directly" into the opponents' goal.

A direct free kick results from any of the following ten offenses, nine of which are committed against an opponent.

The first six offenses must be committed in a manner considered by the referee to be (1) careless, (2) reckless, or (3) using disproportionate force (The Big 3).

Infraction... If a Player...	Comments
1. KICKS OR ATTEMPTS TO	Kicks must be directed only at the ball. The foot "over the ball" kick is considered kicking (CAUTION). If it is viewed as serious foul play, SEND OFF.
2. TRIPS	Stooping in front of or behind an opponent. Tackle from behind: • Ball played with one foot and trips the opponent with the other, DFK/PK • If the ball is played first, followed by an unintentional trip -- No foul.
3. JUMPS AT	• To play the ball is to be looking at it.
4. CHARGES	• If opponent is knocked down, it probably is an unfair charge.
5. STRIKES OR ATTEMPTS TO	SEND OFF, if it is viewed as serious foul play. • Also throwing an object (such as a ball) at a player. • Throw-in made violently at an opponent - Take kick from touch-line.
6. PUSHES	• Usually done with the hands or shoulders.

Things To Remember: In determining fair or foul play, concentrate your attention on the leg nearer to the ball. This is the leg which will often go "across" the ball, and trip the opponent.

The inside leg, closer to the ball, will usually do the damage.

MORE DIRECT FREE-KICKS -- Ball must be in play

The following offenses (four) result in a DFK. However the careless, reckless or disproportionate aspects need not apply.

Infraction... If a Player...	Comments
7. IMPROPERLY TACKLES	Contact is made with the opponent before it is made with the ball.
8. SPITS	Always send off for spitting at anyone... opponent, teammate, spectator or official. Restart with a direct free-kick only if spitting is at an opponent.
9. HOLDS	• Grabbing any part of clothing. • Arm stretched across the chest, retarding the opponent's progress. • Can be done with arm, leg, foot, or torso. Also, two players can "sandwich" an opponent.
10. HANDLES THE BALL (Deliberately)	• Doesn't apply to goalkeper in his penalty-area. • To fall and accidentally touch the ball is not a hand-ball. • The hand is taken to be the whole of the arm, from the shoulders to the fingers. • It is deliberate when a player extends his arms to present a larger target to the ball or deliberately moves his hands/arms toward the ball (hand striking the ball instead of ball striking the hand). • Instinctive movements of the hands or arms to protect against being hit in the face or groin (breast - women) shall not be considered as deliberate handling of the ball. The hands used "palms-outward" is normally a deliberate action. If defensive player scores in his own goal with his hands, the score shall count - ADVANTAGE. • A held object is considered as being an extension of the hand. • A goalkeeper deliberately handling the ball outside his penalty-area or an outfield player handling the ball to deny a goal-scoring opportunity. SEND OFF and a direct free-kick or penalty-kick. • Deliberately handling the ball in order to prevent an attack from developing on a goal. CAUTION. • Handling the ball before it is put into play is not considered a 'Hand-Ball.'

Holding by both players. One's using the hands, the other the body.

LAW XII - FOULS AND MISCONDUCT
DANGEROUS PLAY
(Cautions are frequently administered. The referee has discretionary powers.)

- Restart with indirect free-kick unless it occurs when ball is out of play.
- The referee has discretionary powers regarding a negligent action associated with dangerous play.
    - Player comes to the ball in a manner which is considered dangerous to another player.
    - A player can put himself in danger (e.g., head down at waist level or lower when an opponent is attempting to kick or play the ball. A move normally OK for goalkeeper).
    - Scissors-kick (bicycle, double kick), if it causes another player to move away.
    - Kicking ball or at ball when in possession of the goalkeeper.
    - Heading ball when held aloft by goalkeeper is almost always dangerous play.
    - Goalkeeper or field player lifting knee or leg to fend off an opponent.

    - Stretching out a leg toward the opponent when it could be dangerous to opponent.
- Dangerous play does not have to be committed against an opponent. It can be dangerous even if done against a teammate. If this occurs, you may stop play and give a drop-ball.

Several kinds of dangerous play here. You sort it out.

LAW XII - FOULS AND MISCONDUCT

CHARGING

Fair Charge

A fair charge doesn't have to be weak. It can be hard, but it may not be violent.
In order for a charge to be made fairly, the player:

*   May not have hands or arms extended away from the body.
*   Must execute only with the shoulder against another shoulder; chest, arms, hands, and hips may not be used. A charge must not be made with or against the chest.
*   Must have one or both feet in contact with the ground.
*   If a field player who is not playing the ball and is not obstructing is fairly charged. (Indirect Free-Kick)
*   If a player deliberately turns his back when about to be tackled, he may be charged, but the charge may not be reckless or careless.
*   To look at opponent as you charge him is not playing the ball.

Goalkeeper

The goalkeeper may be fairly charged.

LOCATION	HE OBSTRUCTS	HAS POSSESSION OF BALL	DOES NOT HAVE POSSESSION OF BALL
WITHIN THE GOAL AREA			MAY NOT BE CHARGED (IFK)
IN ALL OTHER PORTIONS OF THE PENALTY AREA			

*   If charged while corner-kick is in the air -- indirect free-kick because he is within his own goal area and didn't have the ball.
*   Unintentional body contact is not to be penalized.

    Goalkeeper may not be charged within his own penalty area. (Youth)

Unfair Charge

    If charged carelessly, recklessly, or with disproportionate force.

Many players believe that referees will not send off a player early in the game. Do what you must, no matter how little or how much time has elapsed. French referee Joel Quiniou sent off a player in the first minutes in the 1990 World Cup.

The ball is a natural cushion and will protect the two opponents in the strongest of tackles. Some *incidental* body contact may result. When the tackle becomes careless, reckless, or dangerous, a foul (and often a caution or "send-off") must result.

LAW XII - FOULS AND MISCONDUCT

CAUTIONS (Yellow Card)

Cause...	Action If Ball in Play	
Player field entry or exit without permission	Indirect Free-Kick	• Apply advantage clause if applicable.
Persistently infringes the Laws of the Game	(As per offense)	
Dissent	Indirect Free-Kick	• Shows by word or movements of the body.
Ungentlemanly conduct	Indirect Free-Kick	• See 'Ungentlemanly Conduct' this chapter.
Deliberately fouling	(as per offense)	
Dangerous play (referee opinion)	Indirect Free-Kick	• See 'Dangerous Play'.
Players (other than the goalkeeper) change shirts.	Indirect Free-Kick	• Require them to change back.
Delaying the taking of a free-kick. (Defensive player wasting time getting back 10 yards from the ball.)		• The Law requires that the opponents be at least 10 yards from the ball. The referee must assert his personality and apply the Laws of the Game.
Field entry by a substitute	Drop-Ball	• If done without permission of referee.

A hard tackle, a Mexican player on the turf at Azteca Stadium (1970), and the first yellow card in the history of the game. Kurt Tschensher of Germany is the referee. Certainly not the first player to gesticulate, "What'd I do?"

LAW XII - FOULS AND MISCONDUCT
CAUTIONS (Yellow Card)

Caution during a penalty-kick if there is an encroachment, the wrong person kicks, or any distraction either to or by the goalkeeper.

If a player receives a third caution during the season, most leagues require him to sit out the next game.

Caution the Second Time in Succession a...
- *Kick-Off* -- is intentionally not played into opponents' half of the field or if there is encroachment by the opposing team. RETAKE.
- *Goal-Kick* or *Free-Kick (within own penalty-area)* -- is intentionally not kicked beyond penalty-area or an opposing player encroaches, or any player touches the ball within the penalty-area. RETAKE.
- *Drop-Ball* -- is touched or played before hitting the ground. RETAKE.

The cautioning of a player takes at least 15 seconds away from play, and sometimes as long as 60 seconds.

Alain Hamer of Luxembourg cautions Heidi Store of Norway. With the left hand he reaches for the red card, as this was Store's second cautionable offense. Perfect mechanics.
Photo by Phil Stephens

LAW XII - FOULS AND MISCONDUCT
UNGENTLEMANLY CONDUCT *(Also Caution)*
All Ungentlemanly Conduct results in a Caution.

Basic

- Restart with an indirect free-kick unless the occurrence involved a penal offense or happened when the ball was out of play.
- Ungentlemanly conduct applies when directed toward opposing players, teammates, referees, linesmen, or spectators. It occurs when the game is brought into disrepute by unexpected or unprecedented behavior, that is, anything that offends the spirit of the game.

Deliberate Hand Ball

- To prevent an attack from developing.
- To make a mockery of the game.

Delaying Tactics

- When in possession of the ball, goalkeeper taunts opponent by withholding the ball from play.
- *Holding ball* -- Goalkeeper holds too long or any player holds the ball with his legs, or intentionally lies on the ball for an unreasonable length of time.
- Defenders not retreating 10 yards for a free-kick or a corner-kick.
  - Do not leave area or are too slow in retiring.
  - Stand on, in front of, or directly behind the ball.

Harassment

- Distracting opponents by dancing about gesticulating, shouting or other actions.
- Jumping in front of a player taking a corner-kick, free-kick, or throw-in.
- Worrying or obstructing goalkeeper. To interfere or attempt to interfere with the clearing move. (May warn on first offense if not blatant.)
- Most attempts to prevent the goalkeeper from putting the ball into play (e.g. attacking player sticks out his leg or hand to inhibit the kick).
- Adopting any threatening posture toward another.

Leverage Used Unfairly

- Leaning on shoulders of teammate.
- Holds onto uprights or to the crossbar to gain an unfair advantage. (Steadies himself to kick the ball or in order to jump higher.)

Field Entry/Exit

- Going off the field or re-entering the field without the referee's permission.
- Substitute enters the field of play without the referee's permission (drop-ball rather than an indirect free-kick).

Injury

- Opponent pulling an injured player from the field in order to humiliate him or pulling him to his feet in order to minimize his injury.
- Faking an injury.

In cautioning, use the card as a confirmation of what you have told the player.

LAW XII - FOULS AND MISCONDUCT
ENTERING/LEAVING THE FIELD

Referee sends a player off the field (Red Card)

Before play starts	May be replaced by a named substitute
After play begins	May not be replaced
At half time	

- If a 12th participant (actually a substitute) enters the field of play and the entry was followed by the scoring of a goal...
- If play has *not* been restarted -- NO GOAL. Resume play with a goal-kick.
- If play has been restarted -- GOAL. Resume play with a drop ball from where the ball was when it was noticed that there were 12 participants.
- Caution the substitute.

TRAINER/COACH UNAUTHORIZED ENTRY

Warn, not caution, the first time it occurs.
Report the incident to match organizers.

PLAYER LEAVES THE FIELD

- Without Permission -- CAUTION and indirect free-kick from where ball was when referee stopped game, if referee stops play to caution. This includes when it is due to disagreements with teammates. The referee may allow the player to re-enter.
- Injury -- May return upon receiving a signal from the referee, even if the ball is in play.
- Equipment Adjustments -- Must present himself to the referee for inspection prior to re-entry.

WENDY ANN TOMS
of Poole, Dorset (England)

"The more you put into the game, the more you receive from it"

One observer put it well: "The wind of enlightened change was blowing through ancient corridors." After nearly 200,000 games and 106 years of soccer, England's Football League assigned their first female official.

It was a hard 10-year struggle, interrupted by a two-month maternity leave in 1985, but Wendy Tom is there. Ambition? That's right. Now that she's in the Football League, she's looking toward the future. "I want to end up on the FIFA list, and to referee in a World Cup match."

Wendy summarizes her thoughts... "We haven't got there by demanding equality and spouting feminism. We prove ourselves on the field of play, as do all referees. Actions speak louder than words."

THE IMITATOR

- Tries to please everyone.
- Calls off-side whenever a defensive player raises his hand.
- Emphasizes a foreign accent.
- Calls obstruction in the penalty-area instead of tripping.
- Calls coach "Doctor" unless he knows his first name.
- Always waits until the linesman flags, then whistles.

THE ROTTENTATOR

- Always needs a shave.
- Has been seen in used clothing stores, rummaging for referee socks.
- Is chronically late for every game.
- Yellow card is so soiled that it's now black.
- Never washes his uniform.
- Wears stolen FIFA patch.
- Shrugs shoulders when fellow official makes an unpopular call.
- Leaves immediately after game, saying he will shower at home.

LAW XII - FOULS AND MISCONDUCT
"SENDING-OFF" (Red Card)

Violent Conduct - When a player is guilty of aggression, even when not challenging for the ball.

May be against an opponent, teammate, referee, linesmen or spectator (on or off the field)	THE BALL MAY BE IN OR OUT OF PLAY

Foul or Abusive Language and/or Gestures.
Being guilty of a second cautionable offense, after having received a caution.

The game is restarted with a DIRECT FREE-KICK or a penalty-kick if the strike or kick offenses are committed against an opponent while the ball is in play. It is restarted with an indirect free-kick in all other situations when the infraction is committed on the field of play (e.g. striking or kicking a referee, linesman, spectator or teammate -- even if in the penalty-area.)

If a Player is Sent Off...
- Before game starts - he may be replaced by a named substitute.
- Any time after play has restarted - he may not be replaced. He may not remain in the bench area, but must leave the general area of play.

Miscellaneous Send-Offs
- Threatening another player in a violent manner.

Serious Foul Play - When a player is intentionally using violence in challenging for the ball.

The tackle from behind with little or no attempt to play the ball.	THE BALL MUST BE IN PLAY
Maliciously striking or attempting to strike or kicking or attempting to kick an opponent.	
Denying an opponent an obvious goal-scoring opportunity through unlawful means.*	

*Examples: Impeding an opponent.
Non-goalkeeper (defender) intentionally handling the ball.
Goalkeeper deliberately handling the ball outside of the penalty-area.

LAW XIII -FREE-KICK (General... Non Penalty-Kick)

Kick, in relation to own penalty-area

Conditions	OUTSIDE	INSIDE	
Where is kick taken?	**AT THE POINT OF INFRACTION EXCEPT:** ...If inside opponents' goal area, must be moved back to the nearest point on the goal area (6 yd) line.	...If within own goal area - any point within the goal-area.	• The ball must be stationary. Taken by any player and in any direction. • Player taking the kick may step outside the boundary lines.
In play	Circumference	Circumference and outside the penalty-area.	• If taken on or near the boundary lines and goes out of bounds before traveling its own circumference - RETAKE.
Plays ball a second time	IFK if ball had travelled circumference, otherwise - RETAKE.	RETAKE (if hasn't passed penalty-area) Otherwise - IFK	
Opponents' distance from ball until it is in play.	10 Yards	10 Yards and outside the penalty-area.	• **Player taking the kick may voluntarily renounce the distance advantage allowed him.** • If an attacking player requests 10 yards and then kicks the ball while the referee is establishing the wall... CAUTION and RETAKE. • If a free-kick is taken within 10 yards of the defending team's goal, the defending players may be on the goal-line between the goal-posts. They must however, have both feet on the goal-line.
Opponent encroachment and referee stops play before kick is taken.	CAUTION		• Unless kicking team takes a quick kick • Encroachment only applies to players of the team that is not taking the kick.
Opponent encroachment and referee unable to stop play before kick is taken.	CAUTION AND RETAKE or Apply Advantage		• If advantage applied, caution player at next stoppage
Goes directly into one's own goal.	CORNER-KICK	RETAKE	• Kick taken from within own penalty-area goes outside of the penalty-area and for some reason comes back and goes directly into own goal (e.g., wind) - CORNER-KICK
Score goal directly against an opponent?	DIRECT - Yes INDIRECT - No: GOAL-KICK		
May teammate be sanctioned for being in an off-side position?	YES		
Ball is kicked to goalkeeper who takes it into his hands within his own penalty-area.	Indirect Free-Kick	RETAKE	

To play a ball is to cause it to move. On free-kick, if the first player to kick the ball does not move the ball its circumference, the kick must be retaken.

LAW XIII - (INDIRECT) FREE-KICK

A goal may not be scored unless the ball has been played or touched by a player from either team other than the kicker before passing into the goal.

Referee signals by raising his arm. It is kept raised until the kick either is played by a second player or the ball goes out of bounds.

The following result in an INDIRECT FREE-KICK...

After putting the ball into play, a player plays it a second time.	If done during the taking of a kick-off, throw-in, free-kick, corner-kick, penalty-kick, or goal-kick going outside the penalty-area.
Off-side	From location of player who was called off-sde.
Ungentlemanly conduct	CAUTION (If the play was stopped for the caution)
Dangerous play (see this chapter)	The referee sometimes cautions.
Goalkeeper takes more than 4 steps with ball	The 4 Step Rule applies until the ball has been played by someone else. It applies while holding, bouncing, throwing the ball and catching it again.
Goalkeeper touches ball with hands.	After ball was deliberately kicked by teammate to him; caution the goalkeeper.
Player uses deliberate trick to avoid kicking ball to own goalkeeper	Caution the kicker.
Fair charges at the wrong moment.	• When not legally or fairly obstructed or ball wasn't within playing distance. • Charging the goalkeeper is allowed except when he is not in possession of the ball within his goal-area. Youth - goalkeeper can never be charged within his own penalty-area.
Dissent with decision by... • Throwing the ball away • Leaving the field • Any other act or gesture of defiance.	CAUTION and IFK if ball was in play.
Illegal Obstruction	If ball is not within playing distance. (Hint - Look at the players eyes and facial expression if possible.) • Using his body as an obstacle. • With or without the ball, he backs into an opponent. • After corner-kick, if opponent then stands in front of the goalkeeper, making no attempt to play the ball. • Running across an opponent's path to retard his progress. • Attempting to prevent the goalkeeper from putting the ball into play (e.g. player standing directly in front of the goalkeeper.)
Restarting game after violent conduct directed against non-opponents such as referee, linesman, spectators or teammates.	Maliciously hitting, spitting or kicking. Foul or insulting language and/or gestures. Send off and IFK if ball was in play.

LAW XIV - PENALTY-KICK

> The calling of a penalty-kick is not an evil act. It is to be done with confidence and with full assurance that you are right. The referee does not create the penalty-kick. He calls it.

A penalty-kick results whenever one of the ten (10) penal fouls is committed by the defending team inside their own penalty-area when the ball is in play. Taken from the penalty-mark (spot) - (12 yards from the goal-line). The ball may not be placed elsewhere, regardless of the condition of the spot.

The referee does not whistle for the kick to be taken until all players are properly positioned. (see below). This includes the goalkeeper having his feet on the goal-line.

It is recommended that the referee hand the ball to the kicker, allowing him to position it on the spot. This also serves to identify the kicker to the goalkeeper.

The referee must verify that no player is outside the field of play or closer than 12 yards to the goal-line.

Correct Positioning

All players except kicker and goalkeeper must be...	In the field of play.	• Kicker may step outside of the penalty-area or the 10 yard arc in order to gain momentum.
	At least 10 yards away from the penalty-spot	
	Outside of the penalty-area	• See encroachment
	At least 12 yards from the goal-line	

The goalkeeper must stand on the goal-line between the goal-posts without moving the feet until the ball is kicked (circumference). If the goalkeeper gets into an improper position on the goal-line after the signal for the kick but before the ball is kicked, the referee awaits the results of the kick.
If no goal is scored - RETAKE. If scored - GOAL.

A goalkeeper may be substituted for on a penalty-kick.

Any player may take the penalty-kick. (This includes the opposing goalkeeper.)

If a penalty-kick is retaken for any reason, the goalkeeper and/or the kicker may be changed. (Note: This does not apply to kicks from the penalty mark to decide a tied game.)

The Kick	Action	
If not in a forward direction	RETAKE	• After the ball is kicked in a forward direction and has travelled its circumference, a teammate may run in from outside the penalty-area and kick the ball.
In play	CIRCUMFERENCE	
The ball is played by the kicker a second time in succession*	IFK	
Ball touches an outside agent. • As goes toward goal. • As rebounds into play.	RETAKE	
	DROP-BALL	
Ball bursts directly on a goal-post or the cross-bar.	DROP-BALL	

*Such as the ball rebounding off the upright or cross bar without the goalkeeper touching it.

HINTS

Quite often a penalty-kick situation results in protest and confusion on the field, and the referee will have difficulty restoring order and may have to caution or send off players on the defensive team. Sometimes it is advisable to pick up the ball immediately after whistling for the penalty, retaining possession until the players from both teams have cleared the penalty-area. The ball should then be given to the kicker for him to place on the penalty-mark in readiness for the kick. This serves to identify the kicker to the goalkeeper. The referee then positions himself, and after both kicker and goalkeeper are ready, he gives the signal for the kick to be taken. With young players it is recommended that the referee remind the goalkeeper to wait until the ball is kicked before moving the feet.

For a strong kicker on a penalty-kick, the ball is in "flight" for .453 seconds before it crosses the goal-line. It takes the goalkeeper 1.125 seconds to reach the upright (corner of goal). Even the best of goalkeepers cannot save a hard, well-placed penalty-kick, unless, of course, his feet have moved before the ball was struck.

Source, "The Football Referee" January 1988

Q: A ball bounces high near goal. A defender and an attacker simultaneously jump and touch the ball at the same time. The attacker had attempted to punch the ball into the goal and the defender attempted to punch it out. What is the ruling?
A: *Both players should be cautioned and shown the yellow card. The referee should resume the game by dropping the ball at the place it was when play was stopped, subject to the overriding conditions of Law VIII.*

ENCROACHMENT

A caution is to be given for all encroachments.

After having whistled for the kick to be taken, the referee does not intervene for an encroachment. He awaits the result of the kick.

Attacker encroachment in conjunction with the goalkeeper moving the feet - RETAKE whatever the result.

| Result | **Encroachment By or Ungentlemanly Conduct......** | | |
	An Attacker	A Defender or Goalkeeper Movement	Attacker and Defender
GOAL	RETAKE	GOAL	
NO GOAL: • Save by goalkeeper or ball rebounds into play.	IFK		
• Goalkeeper touches the ball which goes over the goal-line, but not into the goal.	CORNER-KICK	RETAKE	RETAKE
• Ball goes directly over the goal-line, but not into the goal.	GOAL-KICK		

UNGENTLEMANLY CONDUCT (see chart for Encroachment and Ungentlemanly Conduct)

All ungentlemanly conduct results in a Caution.

The kicker fakes a kick to get the goalkeeper to commit himself by moving his feet.

Distraction by shouting or the making of motions. Normal body movements or swaying are fair. The swinging of arms that are obviously distracting are not.

Player other than the one designated takes the kick (rare).

The player taking the penalty-kick must be properly identified. This is often accomplished by the referee handing the ball to the kicker.

Q: During the preliminaries for the taking of kicks from the penalty-mark, a goalkeeper goes to each of the opposing players, shaking their hands. The linesman informs the referee that this appears to be intimidation. What should be done?

A: *If, in the opinion of the referee, the goalkeeper is guilty of ungentlemanly conduct, the goalkeeper should be cautioned and shown the yellow card.*

At the Taking of a Penalty Kick

- Normal body movements or swaying are fair. The swinging of arms that are distracting are not.
- Player other than the one who is designated kicks the ball.
- The kicker fakes a kick to get the goalkeeper to commit his intention.
- The player taking the penalty-kick must be properly identified. This is often accomplished by the referee handing the ball to the kicker.

Objects

- Goalkeeper (within his penalty-area) hits the ball with an object in his hand.
- Throwing an object at the ball.
- Hiding a dangerous object upon his person (this may also result in a sending off).

Miscellaneous

- To keep playing the ball after hearing the whistle. (See World Cup)
- Making any reference to the religion, morals, or heritage of any individual. This is often considered foul or abusive language, for which the player is shown a red card and sent off.
- Goalkeeper lying or sitting down near his goal as a contempt-showing action when the game is very one-sided.
- Defender going behind his goal-line to create an off-side.
- Defender rushes forward from a wall before the ball is kicked.
- After asking for 10 yards, kicking the ball before the referee has given the signal.
- Players carrying on a conversation "over the referee's head" which indirectly challenges the referee's authority.

THE POTENTATOR

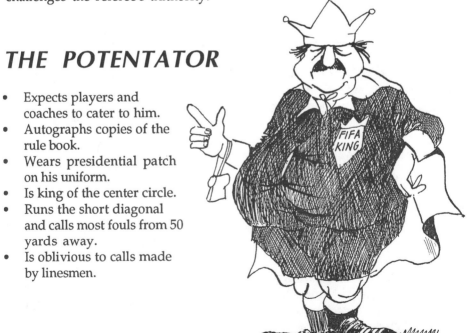

- Expects players and coaches to cater to him.
- Autographs copies of the rule book.
- Wears presidential patch on his uniform.
- Is king of the center circle.
- Runs the short diagonal and calls most fouls from 50 yards away.
- Is oblivious to calls made by linesmen.

TIME EXTENSION FOR PENALTY-KICK
(Referee should notify both captains prior to the taking of the kick that time has been extended.)

When a match is extended to allow a penalty-kick to be taken or retaken (be it at halftime or game's end), the extension shall last until the moment when the penalty-kick has been completed. The players should be cleared out of the immediate vicinity to eliminate possible encroachment and other violations.

Ball

• Kicked out of bounds.
• Kicked toward goal and is clearly saved by the goalkeeper.
• Hits upright or cross-bar and...
      Goes out of bounds.
      Rebounds into play.
• Not kicked strongly enough to reach goal.
• Kicked toward teammate instead of towards goal.
• Hits upright or cross-bar and bursts.
	END OF PERIOD

• Goes directly into the goal • Kicked toward goal, touched by goalkeeper and goes into the goal. • Hits upright or cross-bar or goalkeeper or ground or any combination of these, and goes into the goal.	GOAL & END OF PERIOD
• Touches an outside agent.	RETAKE

Clearly, the referee is watching the kicker during the taking of a penalty-kick. The linesman is at the corner-flag. Five players are encroaching. What are the best mechanics for a penalty-kick? Don't ask why the defender (far right) is facing away from play, showing complete disinterest in the kick. Our guess is that he's preparing for a kick-off or for a counter-attack.

LAW XV - THROW-IN

BASIC	A member of the opposing team last touched the ball prior to it going completely out of bounds (air or ground) outside the touch-line.
WHERE IS THE BALL THROWN INTO THE FIELD OF PLAY?	At the point within one meter of where it crossed the touch-line going out of bounds. If taken at some other point, throw-in awarded to opposing team.
IN PLAY	After it has been released - as soon as it passes or touches any point of the touch-line in flight.
THROWER PLAYS A SECOND TIME	Indirect Free-Kick
SCORE A GOAL DIRECTLY?	NO Thrown directly into opponents' goal - GOAL-KICK Thrown directly into own goal - CORNER-KICK
OFF-SIDE DIRECTLY?	NO
DISTANCE AWAY	• Thrower must be allowed to deliver the ball properly. • If opponents dance about or jump in a way calculated to distract the thrower - CAUTION - ungentlemanly conduct.

The thrower, at the moment of delivery, must...
• Face the field of play with some part of the body.
• Have part of *each* foot on or outside the touch-line and on the ground. (If one or both heels are on the touch-line it quite often will result in a foul throw-in due to the player rising on his toes and losing contact with the touch-line.
  - Feet may be apart.
  - May not deliver the ball while running (both feet in motion).
  - Taken within 1 meter of where the ball crossed the touch-line.
• Use both hands and shall deliver the ball from behind and over his head.
  - Ball must be delivered essentially with equal force and simultaneously with both hands.
  - It may not be delivered with one hand and directed with the other.
• Throw-in is not allowed to be merely dropped, it must be thrown.
  - If a continuous movement, it does not matter at what point it is released.
  - A very 'gentle' throw is *not* considered to be a drop, it is still a throw.

Victory in soccer covers a multitude of shins.

Miscellaneous

Takes throw-in improperly	Other team takes THROW-IN.
Intentionally throws ball away from the field of play	CAUTION - RETAKE
Throw intentionally at referee	SEND OFF - Indirect Free-Kick from the touch-line
Throw ball at an opponent • If as a tactic • If violence against an opponent	OK if done in a non-dangerous manner Direct Free-Kick from the touch-line. SEND OFF
Throw-in hits referee, linesman (if either is in the field of play) or corner-flag. • Remains in play. • Goes out of bounds.	"PLAY ON". Other team takes throw-in

The ball must be thrown into the field of play. If the ball hits the ground before it enters the field of play -- RETAKE.

On the throw-in -- if the ball is not played by any player and...

- It never entered the field of play -- RETAKE.
- It went in and out of the field of play. Other team takes throw-in. Any part of the ball touching or penetrating the outside edge of the touch-line following its release is considered to have entered the field of play. It makes no difference whether or not the ball touched the ground.

TODAY'S WORLD... Dealing with Blood
Suggestions to referees and linesmen

Any bleeding player should immediately be removed from the field until the wound is competely covered. If there is blood on the uniform, have the player change that part of the uniform.

If there is blood on the body, from any source, have the coach remove the player until the wound is cleaned and covered.

The referee and one linesperson should TOGETHER inspect the player and the condition, both before temporary dismissal and after the condition has been corrected.

Each game can bring as many as 2,000 ball contacts, 500 changes of possession, and 100 periods of intense activity.

Law XVI- GOAL-KICK

BASIC	An attacker last touched or played the whole of the ball over the goal-line (air or ground) excluding the scoring of a goal	
WHERE TAKEN	Anywhere within the goal area.	• In taking the kick, only some part of the ball or its projection need be within the goal-area.

IN PLAY	Beyond the penalty-area into the field of play.	• If doesn't go beyond penalty-area or is played by teammate or opponent before leaving the penalty-area. - RETAKE.
		• If crosses the goal-line...
		  - Inside the penalty-area - RETAKE.
		  - Outside the penalty-area - CORNER-KICK

KICKER PLAYS BALL TWICE IN SUCCESSION	Indirect Free-Kick	• If the ball is not yet in play (hasn't left penalty-area) - RETAKE. • If kicker plays the ball a seond time after it leaves the penalty-area.
SCORE GOAL DIRECTLY?	In opponents goal - GOAL-KICK In own goal - RETAKE	• Kick goes beyond penalty-area and for any reason comes back directly into one's own goal (rare) - CORNER-KICK.
DIRECTLY OFF-SIDE?	NO	
OPPONENTS DISTANCE AWAY	Outside of penalty-area until ball clears the penalty-area	• If opponent is trying to leave the penalty-area, let the kick go. The opponent must be trying to gain an unfair advantage in order to be penalized.
TEAMMATES	Any distance.	• May remain inside penalty-area.

The ball must be stationary, but it is quite in order for the kicker to hold down the ball with one hand and simultaneously kick it in order to quickly put the ball into play.

If the ball is deliberately not kicked beyond the penalty-area, or an opposing player encroaches or any player plays the ball before the ball leaves the penalty-area...

- 1st time - WARN
- 2nd time - CAUTION   RETAKE
- 3rd time - SEND OFF

Q: Before the game you discover that the field on one end has a penalty-area that is too narrow. There is no marking device. You call this to the attention of the home team, but start play. During the game an intentional foul is committed, by the defending team, a yard outside the penalty-area line that is parallel to the touch line. May a penalty-kick be awarded?

A: The referee should not have allowed the game to proceed until the penalty-area was correctly marked; however, having allowed the game to proceed, he must accept the markings in making his decisions and may not award a penalty-kick for a foul committed outside the accepted penalty-area.

LAW XVII - CORNER KICK

During a corner-kick, watch the players, not the flight of the ball.

Corner-Kick

BASIC	The defense last played the whole of the ball over the goal-line (air or ground) excluding going into the goal.	
WHERE KICK IS TAKEN?	The whole of the ball must be within the quarter circle at the nearest corner-flag post.	
IN PLAY	CIRCUMFERENCE	
KICKER PLAYS THE BALL A SECOND TIME IN SUCCESSION	Indirect Free-Kick	The kicker is not allowed to play it a second time including if the corner-kick hits a goal-post, referee, or linesman.
SCORE A GOAL DIRECTLY?	YES	Even into your own goal (not likely)
OFF-SIDE DIRECTLY?	NO	
Opponents DISTANCE AWAY	10 YARDS	It is OK for an attacker to place himself in the way of the goalkeeper. Once the ball is kicked, the attacker must move toward the ball. To remain stationary is to obstruct. (Indirect Free-Kick).
Teammates	ANY DISTANCE	

Goalkeeper charged while the kick is in the air...
- Fair charge -- Indirect Free-Kick (Because goalkeeper was within own goal-area and didn't have the ball.)
- Charged violently -- Direct Free-Kick

If the ball crosses over the middle of the cross-bar after having been last played by a defensive player, the referee immediately signals from which corner it is to be taken.

CORNER-FLAG POST

Corner flag-post must not be moved -- WARN... then CAUTION. (To move means to alter from its stationary straight-up position.)

Ball hits corner flag-post and...
- Rebounds into field of play -- IN PLAY.
- Breaks it and ball remains in play -- DROP BALL -- Play is suspended until post is either repaired or replaced.
- Knocks down or tilts the corner-post away from the field of play in a non-dangerous manner -- PLAY ON and correct at first opportunity.

If ball goes out of bounds by knocking down or going over the corner-flag...
- Last played by attacker -- GOAL-KICK.
- Last played by defense -- THROW-IN by attacking team.

Any fouls here? Looks as if everyone's playing the ball. Sort of.

CHAPTER EIGHT

Knowing Fair from Foul

*"Fouls... the vital few, the trivial many.
Make sure you know the difference."*
John Patrick McNaughton

THE TACKLE

"Football is a tough, combative sport."
FIFA Law Book (Additional Instructions Regarding The Laws of the Game)

"There is no such thing as a friendly tackle."
Harry Rodgers

With the exception of the dribbling and kicking of the ball, the tackle is soccer's most frequently used skill. With a combination of timing, aggression, and proper technique, a player can "win the ball" on most occasions by fair tackling. Problems arise for both referees and players when careless, reckless, or overly aggressive (with disproportionate force) tackles occur in play.

Bob Wertz (above) is an experienced referee and currently is Chairman of the National Referee Committee of United States Soccer Federation. Bob has carefully analyzed some of the more common tackles, along with the proper responses of the referee.

TACKLE FROM THE FRONT
Both opposing players are playing in a manner that is not dangerous. Generally, most tackles from the front are fair because they are safe and successfully completed.

-144-

TACKLE FROM BEHIND

No attempt is made by the defender to tackle the ball. This type of tackle is done violently from behind, almost always unsafe and unfair, and the tackler is penalized with a direct free-kick or penalty-kick and sending off (Red Card).

TACKLE FROM THE SIDE

The two-footed tackle with cleats "exposed" or up is potentially dangerous to the leg and ankle of the opponent. At a minimum this type of tackle would be penalized as dangerous play, with a more severe penalty if the defender's cleats make physical contact with the opponent's leg (whether or not the ball is successfully tackled). The defender may also be cautioned depending on the roughness of the play to the opponent.

TACKLE FROM THE SIDE

Very dangerous. The cleats of one of the defender's feet are exposed toward the ball while the other foot and cleats are cleverly aimed at the opponent's ankle or lower leg. Penalty: direct free-kick (or penalty-kick) and possibly a caution for ungentlemanly conduct.

TACKLE FROM THE SIDE

While the leg of the tackler stops the forward movement of the ball, the referee must also watch the foot of the tackler as well. Here the tackler "hooks" his foot around the ankle of his opponent to slow or stop him. Direct free-kick or penalty-kick.

TACKLE FROM THE SIDE

The defender successfully tackles the ball. The attacker merely falls over the ball and the outstretched leg. No foul. Continue play.

TACKLE FROM THE SIDE

The defender tackles the ball from the side of his opponent. The attacker falls over the ball on his right foot, but the defender continues the tackle by putting his cleats into the left ankle. Despite protests of "I got the ball ref," the defender would be penalized with a direct free-kick or penalty-kick and possibly a caution.

CONCENTRATION

"There's nothing that concentrates a man's mind more than the knowledge that he's going to be hanged the next morning"
- Samuel Johnson

Concentration is usually something that is learned, like the Laws. Unlike the player, whose concentration usually breaks when his team loses the ball, the referee can briefly relax only when the ball is out of play. And, as with players, concentration diminishes when fatigue sets in. If you cannot keep up with play physically, you can't keep up mentally.

The "warming up" period for players should be used constructively by the referee. You can learn much from the players at this time: Do they seem well-disciplined? Are they self-motivated, or responding only to the coach? How skilled are they? Merely asking these questions to yourself will cause you to think about the task at hand, and the accumulated bits of information will serve you in the game. It is all part of the "mental rehearsal" that Tom Tutko, noted sports psychologist, talks about in his book, *Sports Psyching*. While Tutko explains what is necessary for the athlete, his words fit the referee as well.

Concentration really begins when you start to imagine what will happen on the field... *"What kinds of fouls are most likely to happen... What is the best position for calling them... What are the most difficult situations for this age group and level... What must I do to properly assess an 'advantage' situation?"*

Of course, you are not to anticipate what is going to happen, but you must anticipate what *can* happen. Unfortunately, most referees go into a game the way some people get behind the wheel of a car... "I won't think about events and demands upon me until they happen." The referee who thinks about refereeing only on the day of the game will seldom improve, and the referee who thinks about the game only while it is being played is also less likely to advance.

Your concentration on all matters of play will lead to confidence. The concentration takes many forms. Very quickly you are able to assess the weak and strong players, conditions of field, support you may expect from fellow officials, influence of crowd upon players, and how you are going to fare at the first stressful moment.

Look carefully for that first foul. How and when you see it and how you handle it will set a standard for the remainder of the game. You should be the first one on the field to anticipate that foul. With concentration, you will know a lot about fouls **before** they happen.

It is possible to hear all, yet respond only to those stimuli which aid you. If a coach says, "Time's up, ref!", don't take a glance at your watch at that moment. Wait, then when the coach is no longer looking at you (he'll not look at you unless you respond immediately), check your watch. It is possible that time *IS* up, but immediate response to such a command is a sign of weakness, and could invite problems. Concentrate on what is said and done on the sideline. At game's end, you should be physically *and* mentally drained.

THE TEN MOST DIFFICULT DECISIONS

There are certain calls (or lack of calls) that have continually plagued referees. In this section, we present our view of the 'top ten'. The judging of the fair tackle, the deliberate hand ball, and endangering the goalkeeper are not to be ignored because these, too, are difficult. We feel that the following present the referee with an even more difficult challenge.

1. LETTING THE GAME FLOW

This is the 'uncall'. "Referee, is thy name nit-picker?" Do you always insist on ball placement for a free-kick on that exact spot? How tolerant are you of a reflexive outcry of a four letter word overheard by only a few and directed at no one in particular? Does every centimeter of the ball have to be within the quarter-circle on a corner-kick? Do you allow a reasonable amount of 'crabbing' along the touch-line for a throw-in? Do you whistle every niggling little foul? Do you react to every dissenting word? Remember, it is often wise to look away and hear nothing. If verbal protests continue, say: "I heard it. There are limits." Can you successfully make the distinction between letting the game flow and the discipline that is needed for game control? The majority of us have trouble, for this is *the* most difficult decision of all. "ALLOW THEM TO CHEAT, BUT NOT TO STEAL."

2. APPLYING THE ADVANTAGE

The advantage must be immediate, clear, and effective. Once you give it you may not change your mind. If you have doubt as to giving it... **don't**! Some referees prefer not to allow the advantage early in the game. The experienced referee has the advantage on a string. He lets it out gradually as the players demonstrate they can handle it and immediately reels it in when nastiness or immaturity is exhibited. When it is applied, there should be a verbal "advantage, play on" to the players accompanied by a signal to both players and spectators that he has noticed the infraction and has chosen to let it pass.

3. THE SECOND CAUTION

How often have you sent off a player when he commits a second cautionable offense? Now ask yourself how often you have done it *prior* to consulting your game card during the booking process. Your mind as well as your notebook should contain the names of cautioned players. Many players exploit the fact that they have a caution because they sense the psychological pressures that are brought to bear upon the referee. To them, the caution doesn't say, "Cool it." It says, "Push the bounds a little bit further." They feel a certain immunity because the typical referee is reluctant to send off unless the action is of a violent nature.

4. THE DOUBLE STANDARD

Almost all of us are guilty of this. When we are, we are allowing defenders to control the game. What is a foul at midfield is often tolerated when committed within the penalty-area. It is a combination of being prudent and lacking the necessary intestinal fortitude. How often have you seen an attacker get "heel nipped" in the penalty area which is just enough to destroy his timing, causing him to shoot wide or not to shoot at all? Have you ever given a penalty-kick for it? Do the players take advantage of you and their opponents when they are within the penalty-area? We have to strive more for consistency. There is no secret formula. Each referee must look within and make the decision for himself. It is possible that the more fouls called in the penalty-area will mean fewer fouls overall.

5. THE OFF-SIDE POSITION

The new wording of the Off-Side Law, adopted in 1995, is a further refinement in an attempt to solve a problem area for many referees and linesmen.

The words "active play" introduce new ways of interpretation, and implementation on the field of play. While all players are actively involved in play simply by being on the field, play revolves around the ball. When the ball is played or touched by a member of one team, usually only one or two teammates are directly involved in 1) interfering with play, 2) interfering with an opponent, or 3) gaining an advantage by being in their position when the play changes its area of activity. If the player is **not** involved in "active play", he shall **not** be penalized for the offside position.

6. TACKLING FROM BEHIND

The tackle from behind usually occurs when a player is beaten. It is also a predictable foul, since the tackler is seen to be moving in desperation, in a "catch-up" situation. Finally, once the tackle takes place, even though the dribbler may retain the ball, retaliation often happens. The tackle brings problems to hesitant referees because (1) often the ball is played along with the trip, and (2) the advantage is sometimes applied. The tackler from behind is in a low-percentage situation. Most attempts from behind should be penalized, for the legs and/or feet are contacted first. The clever player will keep the non-tackling foot raised high, to bring down the opponent, even through the ball itself may be clearly played. More than a free-kick is warranted. A player tripped from behind at high speed can be injured, and a hard trip to a player at any speed results in possible injury. Referees must remember that players who tackle from behind with no intention of playing the ball must be sent off (red card).

7. THE CHARGE

Is it fair or foul? Were both players playing the ball? Where was the ball? Many officials incorrectly penalize the fair charge. If a big guy and a little guy go after the ball, the smaller one may very well end up on the ground. If a player looks at the opponent just prior to charging him, then it is very likely going to be a foul charge. When judging the charge, 'read' intent in the eyes and face and look for non-shoulder contact.

8. DANGEROUS PLAY

Dangerous play is any action that creates a potential or an actual danger to an opponent. If most often involves the 'high kick.' Just the act of raising the foot to chest level or higher does not make it dangerous. It must pose a real threat. The 'bicycle kick' is usually dangerous when it is done in close quarters. The real "guts call," however, is when a player *puts himself* in jeopardy by putting his head down at waist or lower levels close to an opponent who is attempting to kick the ball. How will you call it?

9. OBSTRUCTION
The players who think they know the Laws (usually above 16 years-of-age) will give you more flak about real or imagined obstructions than even the accursed hand ball. A common occurrence of the 'uncalled obstruction', particularly with adult players, is the defender who attempts to 'protect his goalkeeper'. If you see it, call it and give an indirect free-kick.

10. DANGEROUS PLAY OR OBSTRUCTION?
How often in one of your games has a player fallen to the ground, partially withholding the ball from play? It is very likely unintentional and he is thrashing about trying to kick it away. At the same time, an opponent is also trying to kick the ball. Is it obstruction on the player on the ground? Is he guilty of dangerous play because he is putting himself in jeopardy? Is it dangerous play on the part of the opponent? Should a drop-ball be given? Sometimes the situation takes care of itself. Often it doesn't, and you become painfully aware that something must be done. Who gets the indirect free-kick? Whatever you do, do it quickly. Fans and players will accept a quick decision, which must be made to avoid injury.

You will make many decisions as you read the game. Being in the right place at the right time is sometimes a matter of good fortune.

RETALIATION IS A GAME ALL BY ITSELF
by Willy Keo

If there were but one problem in soccer the world over, from the Rose Bowl in California to Wembley in London, to the weekend game in town, it would be inflammatory refereeing. Of course, many decisions bring only 50% acceptance. The whistle never is a 100% pleaser, but we must recognize that some referees are efficient and others are not.

Plagued with the need to "play on", referees often let fouls go uncalled. "Play on" may mean just that, but players' memories are often longer than the referee's, and the "I'll get him!" remains as important as winning the game. The retaliation is seldom the "eye for the eye", and the "trip for the trip." It is often the vicious foul for the marginal pain, the heel-nip for the harmless push off the ball. Looking at the fouls here might help us all to be a little more aware, and to think about these favorites before they happen.

THE BOTHERSOME, BUT NOT HARMFUL

The shirt tug. The slow player who can't keep up often utilizes this one. Retaliation comes quick and sure, particularly at midfield. It seldom happens near goal, for it is too much of a risk of a penalty-kick.

The pants grab. Hands are busy, and will grab whatever is loose in a desperate situation. This intimidation will distract and incense even the coolest competitor.

The early bump. With the hip, back, shoulder, knee, or arm, and usually on air balls, this one is a foul more accepted by referees as if it were a skill and not a violation of "playing the man." Any bump will do, and referees feel its not a foul because it wasn't too hard.

The coaching move. Talking a player off the ball, out of earshot of the referee brings frustration to the violated. How do you detect this? There's nothing better than being close to play.

THE SEMI-VIOLENT

The instep or toe-step. During play, it's sometimes just as easy to step on an opponent's foot as it is to go for the ball. Also, it looks just like the ball's being played. Congestion on free-kicks and crowded defensive walls also bring this on.

Pre-ball and after-the-ball fouling. The ball is played away, and now's the time to get the little dig in, usually a slight, bothersome kick which says, "I'm giving a test to both you and to the ref. What are you going to do?"

THE VIOLENT

The slide tackle. "But I got the ball, ref!" Bordering on the violent, it usually happens from the rear. The element of surprise adds to the indignity of the situation. Getting the ball *and* the legs is all too common. FIFA has directed referees to send off players who tackle from behind with no attempt to play the ball.

The foot-over-the-ball-block. The foot goes over the ball, and cracks the shin of the opponent who is in on the tackle. This is easily a shin-breaker.

FOULS THAT WILL MEAN PROBLEMS FOR YOU

Much of the play in your games is safe, fairly easy to follow, and without incident. However, you will sometimes see players committing fouls that are intentional, dangerous, and which will usually lead to hard feelings and retaliation. Many of the most common ones are depicted here. Think about them and be ready for them. Be prepared to deal with them through superior field position.

The tackle from the side, with the leg crossing over the opponent's.

The foot kicking "over the ball," from the side or front, onto an opponent's shin. Variation: In an exaggerated manner, the player follows through after kicking the ball.

The tackle from behind, where the foot hits the opponent in the achilles area.

The two-footed tackle, where the player jumps over the ball at an opponent.

The goalkeeper jumping at an opponent, lifting one or both legs, presumably to protect himself as he makes the save.

The sliding tackle which misses the ball and catches the opponent in the lower leg or knee.

The late tackle from the side, where the opponent is hit in the thigh. This usually results from a bouncing ball that is not being well controlled by the opponent.

A knee in the thigh from behind, in a feigned attempt to play the ball.

"Making a back" (stopping) in front of an opponent who is legitimately trying to play the ball. Sometimes a player will lean down behind an opponent who is moving backward to play a ball.

The sliding tackle from behind, usually causing damage to the opponent's ankle, and sometimes to oneself. FIFA has instructed referees to send players off who tackle from behind with little or no attempt to play the ball.

A GREAT PERFORMANCE?

How do you know how well you've done in a game? Certainly, the players and coaches don't know. You will have run 4-6 miles, and should be feeling physically and mentally exhausted. You have made thousands of decisions, each in a split second. But, you should have doubts. Were you out of position for some calls? Do you have doubts about some of the decisions you made? These thoughts are natural ones, and not to bother you. NEVER be completely satisfied with your performance, but don't dwell on mistakes. Correct them and move on.

Anything can happen during play. It happened here in 1977, and in the World Cup 17 years later at the same goal in Giants' Stadium. In this case, the goal-scorer (right) was cautioned for ungentlemanly conduct. In celebration of his goal, he swung on the crossbar.

Q: According to the Laws, a coach or spectator may not be carded. How is the referee to handle a situation that would normally be sanctioned by a card?

A: *A coach may be cautioned or told to leave, but the referee should not show the yellow or red card. A detailed report of the incident should be made to the appropriate authority; it is often wise to indicate that the offense was considered as the equivalent of a yellow card or red card offense, as appropriate, and should be treated accordingly.*

In the case of spectators, the referee has the discretionary power to suspend or terminate the game, again making a detailed report of the misconduct to the appropriate authority. Confrontation with a spectator should be avoided. In youth games, it is usually possible to identify to which team the problem spectator belongs, and the referee can ask the coach of that team to explain to the spectator that the game will not continue as long as the spectator's actions are disruptive. If the problem is not resolved to the referee's satisfaction, the game should be terminated.

Sometimes young players will give you a hint about what they think they did.

THE "RICE PUDDING" GAME

Ken Aston has wisely grouped the dull, easy, unchallenging contests into the category of "rice pudding" games. These games, while always containing the possibility of unexpected isolated incidents, make the experienced referee wish he were elsewhere. Challenging the assessor as much as the referee, they do occur, and sometimes frequently.

Some of your games may not present much of a challenge to you. During these games, you can still be challenged, and you can improve. Consider these areas:

1. **COOPERATION.** Use the game to develop special ways of cooperation and communication with the linesmen.

2. **FITNESS.** In a game that is not hotly contested, the ball will not go from end to end as quickly. Experiment with new ways of running. Try longer strides, running backwards, or perhaps being ahead of play more than usual.

3. **MECHANICS.** While concentrating on play, practice a constant eye communication (peripheral vision) with linesmen. It is possible to watch your linesmen without taking your eyes off the play? It can be done, and now may be the time to practice this skill.

In a "rice pudding" game, it's easy to be careless about mechanics.

4. **ATTENTIVENESS.** Listen to everything going on near the touchline and in the field of play. Sharpen you awareness of the banter going on among the players. A referee who says he never hears what's going on both on and off the field is missing a lot.

5. **COMMUNICATION WITH PLAYERS.** Chances are that the players are as bored with the whole thing as you are. Try some new ways of talking with players. One referee we know loosened things up considerably during a game by saying to a halfback during an attack: "I'll race you to the goal-line." Have you ever thought of the facial expression you tote around with you? It might be time to try something new.

Finally, sharpen that attitude, and keep alert. A lot of games explode when all seems well, and almost everyone's asleep.

With just one foul, a "rice pudding" game can turn against you.

Expect the unexpected in your games.

REAL EYE CONTACT...
Have You Thought About It?

There are several ways of using your eyes to accomplish your objectives, both on and off the field.

1. Looking in the general direction of incidents... *"I'm just glancing around, always watching, watching, watching."*
2. Looking directly at players... *"I saw that, and I know you are skilled enough to do better on a tackle."* (This is a routine glance, but giving the message that a player is on notice.)
3. Looking directly at the individual, but with minimal eye contact, because you want to accomplish the task of cautioning, yet not making a big thing of it... *"You've had your warning, and I don't think this is as serious as it might be, but you are in my book."*
4. Looking at the eyes, thus establishing eye contact in a serious situation. You are being very firm. *"You've had it. This is a sending-off offense."*
5. Looking directly into the eyes, to display your earnest desire to resolve a nonviolent problem, such as coach dissent, or in handling a distraught parent or coach when there is a possible injury in a youth game. *"I understand, and I am doing everything I can to work toward a solution here."*

These thoughts are not mind-games, but real tools you can use in asserting your authority and your sensitivity to all that goes on around you.

(All italics above are referee thoughts, not words to players.)

You may disagree with the pointed finger, but the eye contact leaves no doubt about the referee's resolve.

INJURIES

Soccer is not without its injuries, and they may result by means which are fair or foul, sometimes through inexperience and clumsiness, and sometimes through deviousness and premeditation.

The problem facing the referee is how to stop the game at the proper time when an injury occurs in the field of play. A slight injury deserves only token notice by the referee until a natural stoppage occurs, at which time he may stop the game. A more serious injury normally deserves immediate attention and the game should be stopped without delay. When slight injuries occur, and the injured player is not involved in play, wait to stop the game. If his team is at a disadvantage through the injury or the ball is not in play, stop the game. This is especially important when the goalkeeper is incapacitated and the play is suddenly shifted in his direction.

HINTS
1. *When the referee stops play due to an injury, a drop-ball must be given where the ball was when the game was stopped. (Exception: If in goal-area, it shall be dropped on that part of the goal-area line which runs parallel to the goal-line at the point nearest to where the ball was when play was stopped.)*
   Drop-balls within the penalty-area are to be avoided, if possible. Stop play for an injury after the goalkeeper has made his clearing move.
2. *In youth soccer the referee should consider the age of the player in stopping play for injury. Generally, the younger the player, the quicker the game should be stopped.*
3. *Try to avoid touching a player. If he is injured and in need of medical attention, signal for help from a club trainer or coach. Occasionally (usually in youth soccer), a coach or parent will enter the field uninvited. When this happens, wave the person on. After the incident is resolved, remind the individual that in the future he or she will be invited, if needed.*
4. *Do not allow teams to group and refresh themselves during an injury timeout. Make every effort to have the injured player(s) removed from the field so that play may resume.*
5. *Do not allow the team trainer or coach on the field unless you suspect that the injured player cannot attend to himself.*
6. *Do not allow players from either team to crowd around an injured player.*
7. *Do not answer players' queries about the game during this stoppage of play.*
8. *An opponent who lifts a player from the ground to humiliate him and to minimize his injuries must be cautioned for ungentlemanly conduct.*
9. *Soccer injuries, as with ski injuries, are more frequent later in the day, when muscles become tired and reactions slow. Players will sometimes feign injuries at this time to regain strength and wind.*

9.15 METERS, PLEASE!

Make no mistake about it, the administering of free-kicks (and penalty-kicks) is probably the single act which separates the superior from the average referee. Since free-kicks are "set" situations which, if properly executed, result in goals, the defense may use a variety of "gamesmanship" moves to prevent the goal.

Defensive players are required to be at least 10 yards (9.15 meters) away from the ball, or standing on the goal-line between the posts, for the taking of all free-kicks and corner-kicks. The alert referee must know that some players have been coached to distract the offense, delay the game, and generally to cause confusion so the defense may be made ready. This is particularly true with all "ceremonial" kicks near goal, where the wall is being set up and where attacking players may be as confused as the defense. In fact, there often seems to be guesswork on the part of the attacking team... who will take the kick, and how will it be taken?

WHEN THE FOUL IS AWARDED

1. Immediately point the direction of the kick. If it is indirect, raise the arm and say "Indirect kick."
2. Indicate the place where the kick is to be taken.
3. Move away from the play so you will not interfere with a quick free-kick. While you are doing so, if necessary, remind the defense to quickly retreat, or they will be cautioned.

Five time-honored ways of protecting oneself in the wall. It is mystifying that each generation of attackers feels they can gain something by striking directly at the wall.

IF THE ATTACKERS REQUEST TEN YARDS

1. Indicate, "All right, but wait for my signal (FIFA recommends a whistle) before kicking." (They have now reduced their chances for surprise.)
2. Mark it off by quickly running 5-6 steps (or, you should be able to estimate the distance of ten yards within less than 2 feet). Never stride it off. Never push players back with hands or arms.
3. Say, "They're back. They won't encroach." You have significantly reduced the chances of encroachment.

HINTS:

- *If the kicking team has to ask for the ten yards, you probably haven't done your job. Laws XIII, IBD2 and Law XVII require that players retreat, and they cannot be allowed to waste time.*
- *If you stand over the ball and try to move the wall, you are preventing a kick and inviting the defense to defy your own estimate of ten yards.*
- *Be careful about using your whistle to move the wall. You may be whistling when your back is turned on the ball, and some enterprising attacker has sent the ball on the way to the goal. Use your voice.*

THE WALL

Closely allied with the "ten yards" ritual is the wall itself, always set up to prevent an easy shot at goal. Most important is the concept of the advantages which accrue to the attacking team. The attacking team may:

- Ask for "ten yards" from the referee. (They shouldn't have to ask.)
- Take the kick at any time, unless they have asked for ten yards or have been told to wait for the referee's whistle. (Close to goal the referee can tell when a "ceremonial" free-kick is needed without the players asking.)
- Station players within the defensive wall, if space allows.
- Form their own wall, in front of the "ten yard" wall.
- Delay the taking of the kick for a reasonable period of time in order to confuse the defense.

A free-kick near goal, and the referee first handles the ball before turning his back on the attacking team to measure the 10 yards. Advice: (1) Do not handle the ball. (2) Do not STEP off the prescribed distance. Instead, make 5 or 6 short running steps or estimate the distance. (3) Do not turn your back on attackers.

FAIR OR FOUL?

The well-prepared referee must expect the unexpected when a free-kick is awarded near goal. The most common abuses are:

DEFENSIVE PLAYERS

- Players standing over or near the ball to delay the kick.
  Remedy: As already stated, move them back quickly, with a firm voice. Don't threaten them, but caution them if you must.
- All the players in the wall refuse to retreat the proper distance.
  Remedy: Stop the taking of the kick, if you are convinced that the attacking strategy will not be disrupted. Caution one player, and while writing him up, then displaying the card, warn the next player of his fate if he's still there when you complete the first caution. You should stop time. If you do so, make sure they know that these tactics will serve no good, for time is out.
- Players rush at the kicker (the ball) as he moves to kick, and before the ball is in play.
  Remedy: Whistle immediately, before the ball is in play, and then caution. If whistle is late (after the kick), caution, and have the kick taken from the spot where the infraction occurred. If ball goes directly in goal following the offender's action, allow the goal (provided that you haven't whistled), then caution.

ATTACKING PLAYERS

- Occasionally more than one player "runs over" the ball in an attempt to confuse the defense. You may feel this is ungentlemanly conduct. Generally, referees allow this, but remember the attackers must put the ball into play in a reasonable period of time.
- Players try to force their way into a wall. A linking of arms by the defense seems fair, and is generally done to prevent the ball going through the wall. Attacking players in a defensive wall may cause elbowing, pushing, and striking. Discourage this contact through a verbal warning.

FURTHER HINTS

- *An attacking player in the wall is not to be judged off-side if he is even with the second to last defender.*
- *If an indirect free-kick is taken within 10 yards of the opponents' goal, the referee should say, "Defense, ten yards away or on the goal-line." It is usually not necessary to add that players, if on the goal-line, should be between the goal posts. If an infringement occurs, deal with it on an individual basis. Both feet must be on the goal-line.*
- *Young players under 14 have little concept of the wall and of tactics. Show them what is right, and they will comply.*
- *Most problems in the wall can be anticipated. Be ahead of the players in your thinking, and take care of problems before they happen.*

GOALKEEPERS AND THE LAWS

In the eyes of many referees, goalkeepers are privileged. Certainly it is easier to call an infraction in favor of the goalkeeper rather than against him, and experienced goalkeepers know this. Referees should be keenly aware of the variety of infractions in connection with the play near the goal.

Basic Observations:

- Goalkeepers, by nature, are more aggressive than many other players. They see themselves as leaders of the defense. As such, they call teammates off balls in the air and on the ground.
- Goalkeepers occasionally place themselves in dangerous positions. This is allowed because of the requirements of the position in protecting the goal.
- Goalkeepers are skilled with the feet. If they trip someone, it is usually a desperate move.
- Some goalkeepers guard the goal, others the whole penalty area. The wider the range of the goalkeeper, and the more he commits himself, the more likely he is to commit fouls.

Some Common Violations

By Goalkeepers

- Jumping at an opponent, usually over the back. (penalty-kick)
- Raising a leg to fend off an opponent. (dangerous play: indirect free-kick)
- Any foul when a crowded goal area may mean escape from detection.
- Following through on a fisted ball, and striking an opponent. (Striking an opponent, penalty kick, caution, possible sending off)
- A goalkeeper may not prevent an opponent's obvious goal scoring opportunity by deliberately handling the ball outside of the penalty-area. (direct free-kick, with the goalkeeper sent off)
- A goalkeeper may not touch a ball with the hands if the ball has been deliberately kicked to him by a teammate. (indirect free-kick)

By Attackers

- Playing the ball dangerously, even when the goalkeeper is not in possession. (indirect free-kick)
- Jumping at the goalkeeper. Attacker usually coming in at speed, and goalkeeper is vulnerable because he is jumping up, and subject to injury. (direct free-kick)
- Pushing or holding the goalkeeper. (direct free-kick)
- "Innocently" standing in the path of the goalkeeper, usually after a save. (Law 12, IBD 7 is directed toward these players. Player must be cautioned if he persists. (Obstruction and indirect free-kick)
- Obstructing the goalkeeper on corner-kicks, long throw-ins, and on goalmouth skirmishes. (indirect free-kick)
- Turning one's back, and charging the goalkeeper, just after a high ball has been saved. (direct free-kick)

By Teammates

- A goalkeeper's teammate may not use trickery to circumvent Law XII 5C, which prevents the goalkeeper from handling a ball that has been deliberately kicked to the goalkeeper by a teammate. (Caution and indirect free-kick from the place the "trickery" occurred)

Goalkeeper Possession

Goalkeeper possession occurs when one or both hands are preventing the ball from moving. Once the goalkeeper possesses the ball and releases it into play (by putting it on the ground) it may not be touched with the hands until it has been touched or played by an opponent or touched or played by a teammate who is outside of the penalty-area.

Allowed:

- Bouncing with the hand (The four allowed steps counted)
- Throwing the ball in the air and catching it (steps counted)
- Dribbling with the feet (steps not counted)

Not Allowed: (Sanction, Indirect free-kick)

- Tapping the ball along with the hands
- Throwing the ball in the air, letting it hit the ground, then picking it up
- Releasing the ball to a teammate within the penalty-area, who then plays it back to the goalkeeper.
- Touching the ball with the hands after it has been deliberately kicked to him by a teammate.

Goalkeeper Control

If a ball is caught in the air, but lost upon landing, it may be regrasped without sanction. A hard shot, not immediately controlled, may be regrasped without sanction.

Goalkeepers assume a variety of roles. Just after a goal was scored, the referee noticed that the net had become loose. He summoned his nearby linesman, who tried to hook the net back onto its goal. They both tried unsuccessfully, for a fuil minute, while both teams waited. A spectator suggested that they "use the goalkeeper". The goalkeeper was easily lifted, and the problem was solved.

Hint: Make sure that every aspect of your game is conducted safely. And remember, there are many ways to solve a problem.

THOUGHTS ON GAME CONTROL

The problem of game control cannot be over-discussed in referee clinics, and deserves the closest attention of every soccer official.

The success of every soccer referee will largely depend on the attitude he carries with him toward the game and its players. The referee is evaluated from the moment he enters the field of play. He is judged by everyone on his dress, his voice and confidence, and his general demeanor. He should be thorough without reciting the laws, enthusiastic without appearing high strung and nervous, polite without appearing too friendly, and firm while being fair.

The referee's best friend on the field is not his whistle, for his whistle must be used when all else fails. Anyone can blow a whistle, and many fouls occurring in soccer are obvious. Unlike his whistle, his voice will serve him best, and bring him closer to the players. The good referee will never let a hard foul go without a disciplinary word . These warnings help prevent cautions, as cautions help prevent send-offs and send-offs help prevent player riots. These words of advice to a player should always be direct, and positive: "Let's keep the hands down when going for the ball" or "This isn't the kind of tackle I allow," instead of "Don't use your hands going after the ball," or "If you tackle like that again, you'll be cautioned."

Positioning is vitally important when the referee talks to a player. He should not always approach the player directly, for this will call attention to the referee's action. Rather, he should move alongside the player, or he may be moving away from the player while talking. There is no "punishment" involved, and the referee is saying, "I want to get on with the game, but you first must know how I will react to your acts."

Words are administered, if possible, so that both offended and offender can hear. This helps prevent retaliation, and the offended knows that the referee is on the field to protect the players. Even when advantage is allowed, the referee may say, " Play on, watch the tripping, #10." On such an occasion, the referee leaves no doubt that he has seen it, allowed the advantage, and noticed the number of the player who fouled. He has thus gained the respect of both players, and others within earshot, and he probably will not have to warn this player again.

The testing period for the referee is in the first few minutes of each period. If the referee is firm, the testing period will then be over and the players will settle down to a fair game. If the referee fails the testing period, for whatever reason, the game will proceed, but with players waiting for the opening when they can gain the unfair advantage. For the referee, the game is won in these precious minutes. For the players, they must wait the full duration of the contest.

Q: Before a game, you notice the goalkeeper making a mark with his cleats on the field, from the goal line to the 18 yard line, to determine the position of the goal posts. What is to be done?
A: *The referee should caution the goalkeeper immediately for ungentlemanly conduct, and have the mark obliterated.*

FAIR OR FOUL?

HINTS:

1. *Superior field positioning is essential to good game control. Most players will accept a questionable call when a referee is in a favorable position to call an infraction. They will always suspect even an inconsequential whistle if the referee is far from play.*
2. *There are times when the referee is best-advised to keep a distance from players, at the same time requiring them to stay away from him. When a penalty-kick is awarded, dissent usually is prevalent except with the most disciplined of teams. After calling the infraction, and while waiting for players to position themselves, the referee should move immediately to his position at the edge of the penalty area opposite the goal-area line, parallel to the goal-line, where players seldom congregate. He has created distance between himself and the players. If players try to approach him, he may say, "The foul has been called and it is a penalty. I will not change it. If you approach me, you will be cautioned for dissent."*
3. *A smile from the referee should be seen at least once after he has entered the field. This will prove he is human. Too many referees assume their responsibility with never a smile nor a bit of humor. This method can break the tension in a game, but should never be attempted when it could be misconstrued as being at the expense of a player.*
4. *The referee's main responsibility lies in protecting Law-abiding players from those who disregard the Laws.*

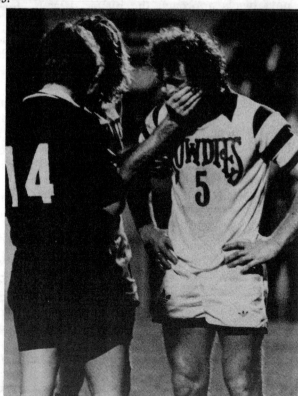

Although this could happen in your game, don't depend on players to help your game control.

WISDOM FOR CONTROL
30 seconds of time = 30 minutes of harmony

Many times you will experience opportunities for communication with coaches. When an occasion presents itself, think positively, take a deep breath, and make the most of it. When you perceive a direct challenge to your authority, you must react. Here's what you need to do:

1. Stop the game by blowing your whistle. Stop the watch and claim the game ball. (When you have the ball, all attention will be on you.)

2. Run toward the area where the coach is located, making sure you walk the last few yards. If you feel you need time to rehearse your words, walk the whole distance. TAKE YOUR TIME!

3. Invite the coach a few yards into the field, where no words can be overheard. The only exception: you may want a neutral linesman to be part of the conversation, but only if you feel that your words may receive an inflammatory response. A linesman's presence accentuates teamwork.

4. Be cool. Remind the coach of his responsibilities, and of your own. Try to reach an understanding. Control the conversation. Ask for cooperation. Do not justify calls or a game situation. If you are ENTIRELY confident that he is about to cooperate, you may want to place a hand on his shoulder. You may also want to write something down in your notebook after you have parted ways. He will have no idea what you have written, but this is effective as a reminder to you both that an incident occurred.

5. Pick up the ball, which you may have chosen to leave at your feet, and run to the place where the game is to be restarted. Restart your watch, blow the whistle, and continue the game.

A wise referee processes the sideline banter, and knows when to seek some harmony.

"A PHYSICAL GAME IS NOT NECESSARILY A DIRTY ONE"
Sam Foulds (1908 - 1993)

The fence you must straddle between fair or foul in a soccer game has no equal in sport. FIFA frequently reminds referees that the unintentional foul is not a soccer crime and therefore should not be penalized. This is fine in theory, but is not necessarily practiced. Your decisions and interpretations are based on judgement. Common sense must prevail. It is genuinely the intent of some players never to foul, but the foul is rightly called. It is the intent of others to foul, and they think of NOTHING ELSE five yards away as they close the gap on the opponent. The yellow card is in order. While you must be sensitive to the demands of the Law, you should also be aware of the demands of the competition you are officiating.

Soccer in America did not begin in the late 1960's, when youth programs introduced thousands of parents to the game, and when foreign players started looking longingly to our shores. Rather, it began 100 years ago, where legitimate safe physical contact was a part of its character. The British influence was total. Now, the modern game brings Third World, European, and South American influence, where skill, footwork, and semi-direct moves (call them indirect) to goal disdain hard physical play. American players are robust and forceful. This is a trait that is evident in the American character. This character emerges on the field, and referees must be highly sensitive to it. *The hard player, within the Laws, must be allowed to see an opponent fall without fear of interruption from the referee.*

It helps if you play, or did play the game. Your questions should always be, "Is the intention to play the ball or the man? He can't do both!" Players can disguise a foul, and others are called just for being hard. One key element that lends vitality to dull and docile games is the fair *shoulder* charge. This miscalled "violation" can be an application of physical contact without being dangerous. It is legitimate, and an effective approach for obtaining the ball in a tight situation. It is a lost art in present-day soccer. The foul should result only if the player is charged, in the wrong place, at the wrong time, or violently. *Violence is a matter of degree, difficult to measure.*

More discussion in referee meetings and clinics should be directed to the fair charge and to the fair tackle. What is needed is not a new definition of violence, but an understanding of the real nature of fair play. Professional indoor soccer, a throw-back to the old days (when the Laws were the same as they are today) is bringing physical contact and zest to the outdoor game. Skill and physical action exist side-by-side, just as the indoor and outdoor games can complement one another. When does a nudge become a charge, and when does a charge become violent? You decide! *The skill of a physical action is just as worthy as the skill of a non-physical one.*

Contrasted with the sly moves of players who tend to intimidate by foul means, the open, fair, physical move to play the ball is for all to see and appreciate. Referees remember... *"A physical game is not necessarily a dirty one."*

HOW TO CONTROL A PHYSICAL GAME

Before the game starts, know all you can about the teams. Is this a rivalry? What is the reputation of the teams? Don't decide before the game that you will "get tough" or "go easy". Let the players decide their own fate, but be ready. Soccer is a physical game. Don't panic because it gets a little rough. Sometimes it is good to keep play moving immediately after a foul. However, if the intensity level is too high, use some delay tactics:

1. After a foul, tell the players to wait for the second whistle. Walk to the players, say what is on your mind, then walk away. This 20 second "interval" will often calm players.
2. Address the player who is fouled as well as the one who fouled.
3. Slow the game down to show all that you're giving everyone time to think. Walk to one or both of your linesmen to have a discussion. Have a prearranged signal for this discussion. The fact that you are meeting may be enough for players to regain their composure.

SIGNS OF IMPENDING VIOLENCE	*REMEDIES*
Verbal abuse of opponents	*Warning or caution or send-off*
Baiting of or gesturing to opponents	*Warning or caution or send-off*
Fouls that go beyond the physical	*Caution or send-off*
Questioning of calls by coaches and players	*Warning or caution*
Players who create fouls, then wait for	*Move quickly to*
retaliation, rather than retreating.	*location of foul*

"Let's drag him over there, away from the free-kick."

WARNINGS, CAUTIONS, AND SEND-OFFS

"Watch for big problems. They provide big opportunities."
- Thomas Wharton, Scottish referee

The consistent and disciplined attitude of the referee is best exemplified in the handling of warnings, cautions, and send-offs. Since the referee whistles the game not only for the players or spectators, but also to apply the Laws of the Game, immediate and effective measures must be taken when disruptive acts or persistent infringement of the Laws take place.

Law XII states clearly the conditions under which players must be cautioned or sent off. These conditions should be memorized, as you must be prepared to give your reason for "carding" players. The referee should not hesitate to adhere strictly to the conditions of the Law. He should also be aware of all options during these opportunities.

The word "warning" appears nowhere in the Laws, yet it appears frequently in referee discussions, and on the field of play. Do not confuse warnings with words and other banter that sometimes is heard from referees and players. Warnings do not need to be in the form of words. A shake of the head and a stern expression is a silent, but sometimes efficient warning. Many successful referees talk their way through games, constantly issuing friendly advice and tips on fair play. While it may be most unusual to stop play for the issuing of a warning, it may be an effective tool as you seek to gain control. You may elect to talk with a player, even making a note of it on your game card, and proceed without a caution. This is a firm and efficient way of conveying your message to everyone. It might be called a "ceremonial warning." If you should do this, play would have to be restarted with a drop-ball.

Most players accept cautions as a definition of the limit that has been set by the referee. The conditions of the game and your experience will guide you. Cautions can come in the first minute, or even at halftime, as it did in the 1974 World Cup Final with Cruyff being shown the card on the way to the dressing room. You may wish to first talk with the offended player before your caution. This preventive measure may avoid retaliation, and will slow things down for the game control that you desire.

The sending off of a player is almost always a ceremony, and usually an unpleasant one. Other players want to know you are in control, and most will respond positively if the red card is shown quickly and affirmatively. To avoid confusion, always face the player being carded, making sure you are far enough away to avoid the risk of a frustrated player swiping at, or taking the card.

The red and yellow cards were the idea of Ken Aston, who in observing the reactions of some players in the 1966 World Cup, found that the players had been "booked" (cautioned) without their knowledge. The cards were introduced in the 1970 World Cup in Mexico, in an effort to communicate disciplinary measures and to surmount language problems. The cards are now used throughout the world and written into the Laws. They have also been adopted by other sports as diverse as water polo, field hockey, and volleyball.

THE UNIVERSAL EXPERIENCE

It happens to every referee, early in the career. First there's a foul, some minor dissent, then a retaliation foul. Then words on both sides, some from players who weren't even involved. Players soon lose concentration on the ball, fearing still another foul, and protect themselves by the raised knee or the foot over the ball. The ball becomes secondary and players will soon deal with the referee's loss of control on their own terms. The words are ugly, and the big explosion isn't far away. Several players may be sent off and the game will not reach an acceptable conclusion.

In his initial year as a referee in Israel's First Division, Abraham Klein analyzed his own performance in a game that ended early: "It was my fault. It was bad refereeing. I vowed it would never happen again."

Here's what he decided:

- Firmness must begin with the referee's first contact with players. This may even be in the dressing room.
- Be closest to play in the early stages. **Do not apply the advantage.**
- Allow no dissent that can be heard by others.
- Whenever possible, communicate with the player who is fouled, as well as the guilty one. This can sometimes be done with simple eye contact.

Just one unpunished foul can turn your game into a very forgettable experience.
From: "The Referee's Referee," by Abraham Klein and Rubi Shalev.

Q: A star player, an attacker, is repeatedly fouled, but each time be a different member of the opposition. What can the referee do?
A: Referees have the responsibility of identifying those players who might be "targeted" by their opponents and must protect them from being fouled excessively. Once the referee has identified this as a problem, he should make it clear that such continued action will be considered ungentlemanly conduct.

SOME WORDS ON OBSTRUCTION

Obstruction can be fair or unfair. If the ball is within playing distance (usually on the ground and about 3 feet away), a player may fairly obstruct an opponent. Unfair obstruction, however, is the often deliberate action of one player which impedes the progress of an opponent. There are times, often around the ball, when an opponent's progress can be slowed just enough to make the move effective, but unfair. You also may see a defender "planted" and unable to avoid the quick and clever movement of the attacker. The defender is sometimes wrongly called for obstruction.

Here, the attacker, #7, has played the ball through the legs of an opponent. This is called "nutmegging."

Before the defender can react, the attacker has committed a careless charge. This is often wrongly called obstruction on the defender. The correct call is for unfair charging, and an indirect free-kick should be awarded.

WHAT TO DO AT HALFTIME

Law VII states that halftime shall not exceed 15 minutes, except by consent of the referee. If, due to special circumstances, the referee deems it necessary to extend the halftime period beyond five minutes, he will probably meet with little resistance, for this period usually lasts ten to fifteen minutes.

Some experienced referees have the habit of announcing, upon the period's end, that "Time is up... 15 minutes between halves." They will then immediately start timing this interval, and will reconvene the players about twelve minutes later, allowing a minute for re-assembly and organization of the two teams. This establishes the referee's authority even during halftime, and allows no extra time for rest.

The referee should be seen only with his two neutral linesmen at halftime. They should not expect refreshment from either team. They should not discuss the game with managers, players, coaches, or spectators. This valuable time is to be spent exchanging mutual constructive criticisms on the progress of the game.

Probably the singlemost important topic at halftime should be a discussion of players' behavior and play. If there are problems or anticipated problems (the second half invariably presents more of a challenge than the first), they should be discussed. Warnings, cautions, and ejections should be discussed in detail. Often referees are seen at halftime with seemingly little to discuss. Two topics should be in mind: (1) "What did we do in the first half?" and (2) "How are we going to do in the second half?"

HINTS

1. *Always retain the game ball at halftime, for you are responsible for the ball until game's end.*
2. *During the 15 minute interval, have the linesmen re-inspect the nets, which may have become loose with halftime activities.*
3. *Never be afraid to ask your linespersons at half time if they are noticing things on the field that you are not. If so, it is their duty to report them to you.*
4. *If the linespersons are doing their job, they should be complimented at halftime by the referee. If they are not, the referee should try to be constructive in his approach to them. The referee needs their support, for an uncooperative linesperson can destroy the efforts of the best referee.*
5. *Be extra alert during the opening minutes of each half. This is the time when players will test your alertness and your strict enforcement of the Laws of the Game.*
6. *Smoking presents a negative image to coaches, players, and other referees. Refrain from smoking at halftime. (The American Youth Soccer Organization does not allow their referees or coaches to use tobacco products during practices, games, or in the immediate vicinity of the soccer fields.)*

HINTS DURING PLAY

- *Obvious fouls need only the whistle. Everyone knows what has happened. Don't point or gesticulate.*
- *Subtle fouls, such as an obstruction, or a charge, need a definite, clear, and immediate signal for the direction of the kick. Walk or move quickly away from the player (unless you sense possible retaliation), for you will no doubt have the possibility for dissent in such decisions. Players seldom consider the possibility that you are right.*
- *Get the habit of walking or moving in the direction of the kick. This shows the offenders that the kick will be taken toward their goal.*
- *A hand signal indicating direction of kick is proper. However, do not keep it up after players have fully accepted the direction.*
- *Do not get in the habit of pointing where the ball should be placed for a kick. "over there, near the bare spot" is enough.*
- *Pointing to the goal area and the corner area for kicks is recommended, but when everyone knows what's happening, you need only to move toward your next position.*
- *A penalty-kick, always unwelcome by the defense, demands your pointing to the penalty-mark. Do not run to the penalty-mark.*
- *Keep the "Play on, Advantage" signal to a minimum. Usually no one is looking and no one cares. In most cases you may be trying to justify not calling a foul.*

If you see a bad situation developing keep the ball moving before things get worse.

Q: A goalkeeper screams at his teammates following their mistakes that lead to a goal. No foul language is used. Is this ungentlemanly conduct?
A: This might possibly be considered ungentlemanly conduct, depending on its extent and duration; it is generally accepted practice to allow such conduct, unless it becomes excessive.

Q: A foul has been called. The referee signals with the arms and hand for the defense to retreat 10 yards. Before they retreat, the attacking team takes a quick kick, and it is intercepted just a yard from the ball's original location. Is the kick to be retaken?
A: Unless the referee has told the team taking the kick to wait for his signal, the kick should not be retaken and play should be allowed to continue.

STILL MORE HINTS:

- *Referees should go toward players to administer cautions and send-offs. To stand your ground and require players to come to you is to abuse your authority.*
- *All cautions and send-offs must be recorded, along with the name of the offender. Also include the offense and the time elapsed.*
- *A player who has been sent off must leave the bench area.*
- *If an expelled player returns to the field, he is no longer considered a player.*
- *Angry people do not make good decisions. Stay calm. Do not look, appear, or act angry as you card a player.*
- *Some referees will communicate with the coach as they run by the bench: "Number 12 is close to being carded." A wise coach will act on this information.*
- *Referees should routinely be more concerned by what players do than by what they say. You may hear everything, but you do not need to react to it.*

When I caution a player, I tell the player of my future expectations rather than dwelling on the past. I ask if there is going to be a change in behavior, and wait for an answer. I have never had a problem with a player who committed to a change."
- Daniel T. Barrett, Member, AYSO National Referee Commission

---

*Fortunately, this is
a very rare scene today.*

There's seldom an advantage on high balls in the penalty-area.

CHAPTER TEN

Don't Just Do Something... Stand There!

"What is this life so full of care,
We have no time to stand and stare?"
W. H. Davies

THE ADVANTAGE CLAUSE
"It must be clear, immediate, and effective."

The advantage clause is a very effective tool for the referee, for it allows him to ignore the whistle for the good of the game.

Law V states that a referee may "refrain from penalising in cases where he is satisfied that, by doing so, he would be giving an advantage to the offending team."

The advantage clause is self-explanatory. Contrary to the "no harm, no foul" situation in basketball, there can indeed be harm, but as long as the offended player or team will retain the advantage, or have more of an advantage by retaining the ball without game stoppage, no foul is called.

The correct application of this clause within Law V is most difficult for the inexperienced referee, and real understanding of its meaning will come only through extensive game experience. The new referee should know that he can only *assume* what *might* happen if he allows play to continue, and that he is always technically right by ignoring the clause and whistling for all violations, regardless of the position of the offended. Most qualified referees admit that in cases where extreme discipline problems prevail and when a player may retaliate for an unpunished offense, it is always better to call the foul and ignore the clause.

An infraction, and advantage signalled... or is it?
While possession is maintained, two opponents are close, and closing in.

Generally speaking, the more advanced the level of the game, the more the advantage clause will be applied, for the players will expect it. In lower levels of soccer such as youth competition, the official should endeavor to teach the players that all fouls are unfair, and must be penalized.

HINTS

1. *In applying the advantage, it is always advisable to acknowledge having seen a foul. The recommended signal is to wave the arms and hands at waist level with a verbal indication of "Play On, Advantage." This will indicate to both players and spectators that you have noticed the foul.*

2. *Once you have elected to apply the advantage, you may not change your decision, even though a player may stop play, lose his own advantage, and ask for a whistle.*

3. *When in doubt, do not use the advantage. The player or his team must have clear possession and the clear advantage that he had before the infraction.*

4. *Early in the game, apply the advantage only when a direct scoring chance is evident, but not at midfield. After the authority of the referee has been established, a more liberal application of advantage may be used.*

5. *In a hard-fought game where extreme contact is frequent, it is often advisable to neglect the advantage as a preventive measure to keep the game in control.*

6. *If the advantage is applied, and a sanction is in order, the referee should wait until the ball is out of play to caution unless circumstances require immediate action.*

7. *The advantage may also be applied when a player is fouled but a teammate obtains or retains control of the ball and it is clearly to the fouled team's advantage to let play continue.*

8. *On a foul that takes place in the penalty-area, the referee should apply the advantage clause only if he is almost certain that a goal will be scored.*

9. *The referee must be more concerned about the effect of an illegal act than about the act itself.*

10. *Use advantage to your own advantage, never to your disadvantage.*

Be careful about the advantage with soccer's youngest players.

THE "OTHER" ADVANTAGE

The "other" advantage has to do with practical game flow, but most of all with good common sense.

Law V IBD 8 says,

> *"The Laws of the Game are intended to provide that games should be played with as little interference as possible, and in this view it is the duty of referees to penalise only deliberate breaches of the Law. Constant whistling for trifling and doubtful breaches produces bad feeling and loss of temper on the part of the players and spoils the pleasure of spectators."*

The common interpretation tends to be to not whistle so many 'ticky-tacky' fouls. This in part is a correct interpretation, however it is often used as carte blanche for doing nothing. This occasionally results in chaos.

V-8 is difficult to implement properly, possibly more difficult than the advantage clause.

As the flow of the game goes, so goes your game control. It, like the advantage, takes on more importance as you officiate the older and more experienced player. V-8 can't be taught. It comes only with a continued awareness of it... and much experience.

SIGNALING A FOUL WITH REPEATED BLASTS OF THE WHISTLE

Everyone's attention is drawn toward you. It distracts the players' concentration. One of the worst things it does is to diminish the effect of the whistle when it is really needed.

Law VIII   Every player shall be in his own half of the field and opposing players not less than 10 yards from the ball until the ball is kicked off.
Ask yourself as a referee, "Is an advantage being gained?" If not, then call the kick back only if the encroachment is blatant. Failing to do so might cause your credibility as a referee to be questioned.

Law XI   Off-side position, but goalkeeper can easily play the ball first.
This has to be used very carefully. Many referees feel that it aids game flow. If the referee discovers that he made a mistake by not calling the off-side, he may still redeem himself with the late whistle... because the moment of judgment extends until the next moment of judgment.

Law XII   If the goalkeeper takes more than 4 steps when holding, etc...
The purpose is to prevent the goalkeeper from wasting time. As long as you are convinced the goalkeeper is attempting to put the ball into play, don't count stutter steps or be overly picky about the number of steps taken. You may also tell the goalkeeper to "watch" the steps.

Law XVII *The whole of the ball shall be placed within the quarter circle.*

Is a player gaining an advantage because the ball is not 100% within the area? If you think so, then don't allow the kick until the situation is rectified. The main thing is that you don't require the letter of the law just because you are aware of its existence.

Your fellow official makes a non-serious mistake.

If possible, do not correct it until halftime or at game's end. For example, your linesman may point in the wrong direction.

If the players, coaches, or spectators don't make a big deal out of it... why should you? On-the-spot overruling should only be done for a reason... and not merely to assert your authority or Law knowledge.

Probably the most notable aspect of the "other" advantage is the...

EXACT BLADE OF GRASS SYNDROME!!

Law XII *A free-kick is awarded to the opposing team from the place where the offense occurred.*

How many times have you seen an over-zealous referee run over to a spot and *demand* the ball be placed at that exact location? How many times have you seen him require that the ball be meaninglessly moved a yard or so to comply with the referee's requirement? If an off-side occurred within 30 yards of the goal of the team taking the indirect free-kick, who cares if the ball is played 5-6 yards forward or back? Who cares if the ball is displaced laterally by 10-15 yards as long as no advantage is being gained? Only the officious referee.

There are instances, however, not to be casual about:

- Defenders usually would prefer that the ball be placed just outside of the penalty-area as opposed to within. Don't compromise. If the foul was committed within the area, have the free-kick taken from inside the area.
- Don't ever let an off-side near the halfway-line result in the ball being kicked from within the offender's own half of the field.
- If one player is off-side and another player is merely in an off-side position, make sure that the ball is placed in the immediate vicinity of the psoition of the player who was whistled for being off-side. If not, you will be chipping away at your own credibility.
- The closer to the goal that a foul is committed, the tighter the referee should become regarding ball placement.

The placement of the ball for a foul that is committed near midfield or by the attacking team in the defender's territory should be given the same latitude as the routine off-side.

Law XV *The ball shall be thrown in from the point where it crossed the line.*

Does the thrower's team gain an unfair advantage? If he 'crabs' a few yards in either direction...

- at midfield... Probably not.
- close to the opponent's goal?... YES, if in the direction of the opponent's goal (an unfair advantage). However, an advantage *can* be gained in either direction.
- close to his own goal?... YES if it puts him within throwing range of his own goalkeeper (an unfair advantage). However, an advantage *can* be gained in either direction.
- Law XV, IBD 4 is basically to prevent time-wasting on throw-ins when players deliberately take the throw-in at an inappropriate location. Throw-ins should be taken quickly and within a reasonable distance of where the ball totally crossed the touch-line.

There are two questions you must ask yourself.

1. *Is a team being taken advantage of? This you should not allow.*

2. *Am I being taken advantage of? We make ourselves look bad enough without having to be helped along by the players. Don't be officious, but don't let them do a number on you either.*

"He tripped himself, ref."

THE TOUCHTATER

- Before game, asks referee who is senior linesperson, in the event the referee becomes incapacitated.
- Carries extra folded-up flag in right sock, but doesn't know why.
- Ignores coach asking for substitution because she was told not to listen to coaches.
- Will not permit coaching or cheering from side-line area.
- Carries three pouches of lime in pockets, to "tidy up" the touch-line.
- Shouts at referee during play, asking him if he's tired.

- Moves people back from touch-line in any way that's convenient.
- Instructs 16-year-old players on the correct method for taking throw-ins.
- Gives "thumbs up" signal to referee each time the whistle blows.
- Stops game to ask referee about a question she missed on the last test.
- Has written the words "DON'T BOTHER ME!" on the back of her collar.
- Ten minutes before halftime asks the coach to prepare refreshments, indicating her preference.
- Has oversized red and yellow cards protruding from rear pockets, and points to them when she hears spectators whispering on the sideline.

When it begins again, you may be faced with a challenge... and sooner than you think. English referee Jack Taylor (with ball) just prior to the 1974 World Cup Final, Germany vs. Holland in Munich. In front of the home supporters, Taylor whistled a penalty-kick before Germany had even contacted the ball. Eighteen Dutch passes, then Cruyff went into the penalty-area. A whistle, a penalty, then a goal, in the most dramatic opening of a World Cup game.

CHAPTER ELEVEN

After It's Over, Before It Begins Again

"No one can make you feel inferior without your consent."
Eleanor Roosevelt

Referee: "Do you have an assistant coach?"
Coach: "Yes. Why?"
Referee: "You'd better warm him up."

REFEREEING THE REFEREES

"If the intent is to criticize, don't do it. If it is to help, do it."

The late Jimmy Walder was once asked how many times he was "assessed" during his more than 50 years with the whistle. "Each game," he mused, "and the total number of assessments depended on the number of people that were watching the game." Actually, Walder was never assessed. He officiated in an era where each referee was on his own, and the only help came from within. Assessment for soccer referees is now a reality, and efforts by many groups are being made toward standardization.

Though a single sheet of paper can be the assessor's report, the most valuable tool the assessor brings to the task is his attitude. Objective criticism of another's performance is a highly sensitive issue, but can be the major force in a referee's development. The assessor is just one part of the officiating team, and his chief job is to help. There are various ways of quantifying performance, and it is felt that providing officials with a "score" needs careful examination. Instead, the intent here is to present some basic observations on elements common to the task of controlling a soccer game.

Referees learn from each other. From left: George Cumming, Development Director, Scottish Football Association, Leslie Mottram (Scotland), Peter Mikkelson (Denmark), Joel Quiniou (France), and Brizio Carter (Mexico). All except Cumming officiated at the 1994 World Cup.

A BRIEF GUIDE FOR ASSESSORS
Key elements for judging a performance...

- **APPEARANCE.** The purchase and maintenance of a good uniform is required. What first impressions does this referee create?
- **SIGNALS.** A demonstrative referee is compensating for weaknesses. Do the signals indicate confidence and does the whistle speak with authority, and is it varied?
- **STOPPAGES.** When the ball is out of play, trouble can begin. Is the game quickly, fairly, and accurately restarted?
- **THE ADVANTAGE.** Does the referee have a real feel for the advantage, using it neither too little nor too much?
- **COOPERATION WITH LINESMEN.** The "team" concept begins with pre-game instructions, where linesmen are given responsibility and respect. It carries over to all other aspects of handling the game. Do eye contact and signaling show that communication is evident in all situations?

In determining the denial of an obvious goal-scoring opportunity (Serious Foul Play), the referee must consider the following:
    Location of the foul and of the defenders.
    Direction of play.
    Proximity of the ball.

On the touchline, at least 30 yards from the diagonal. The referee goes where he must. The whistle in the mouth? Old habits are hard to break. What would you say to this referee?

- **APPLICATION OF THE LAWS.**
  The Penal Offenses. Does the referee really understand the difference between "careless and reckless" and "incidental" fouls?
  Non-Penal Offenses. Dangerous play and illegal obstruction are determined by the referee's perceptions of what is dangerous and of what may be "impeding the progress of an opponent" rather than normal, fair obstruction. Does he understand when these are extreme enough to be called?
  Misconduct and Game Control. Some referees often appear to be interfering with play, and create hard feelings. Is he looking for trouble in areas where it is better to turn the blind eye? Are situations dealt with fairly and quickly?
- **GAME CONTROL.** Are the players accepting decisions? If not, what is being done to correct this dissent? Does the referee appear to understand the game and all that is going on around him?
- **POSITIONING.** A basic problem of referees is the apparent inability to move off the diagonal to the play, and to be looking in the right place at the right time. Does the referee appear to anticipate incidents?

REFEREES AS SPECTATORS

Why do you find yourself, as a spectator, often disagreeing with the referee on the field? As a spectator, you:

1. Are usually farther from play, and unable to judge situations.
2. Are often not at field level.
3. May be supporting one team.
4. Cannot hear the sounds of the game.
5. May respond to biases around you.
6. Are watching the game for pleasure, not for judging play.

The hat and sunglasses help against the setting sun. The line-up card in hand, the fanny pack (not easily seen), the watch and whistle on the neck lanyard and the coach on the touch-line provide ample opportunities for a post-game evaluation. What would you say to this linesman?

WRITING GAME REPORTS

*"The average soccer referee does not render a good report.
It is perhaps the most neglected aspect of referee training.."*
- Pat Smith, formerly Chief Assessor
North American Soccer League

Referees dislike paperwork, and would rather talk about incidents than take matters to the proper authorities through a report. The writing of these reports is probably the most unwelcome task of the referee. Most league rules require a reporting of all incidents resulting in yellow and red cards, and for good reason. These reports form the "word picture" of what actually happened. The report, usually acted upon at a hearing or some other meeting, must contain all of the elements of the situation.

ELEMENTS OF AN EFFECTIVE GAME REPORT

- **PUNCTUALITY.** The reports should be legibly written and mailed immediately following the game, when the facts are clearly in mind. A copy should be kept by the referee.
- **ACCURACY.** Names, numbers, time, score, and the citing of the Law which was violated are all vital to the report. A sketch of the field may help, if you feel this is important. If foul or abusive language is involved, include it in the report.
- **BREVITY.** No one wants to know the full history of the game or players in question. Don't build a case. Just say what happened.
- **HONESTY.** The referee must deal only with the incident, and must not "invent" circumstances which support his position.
- **UNIFORMITY.** Although no two persons see the same incident alike, credibility is there if the incidents were similarly viewed and interpreted by referee and linesmen.

HINTS
1. *Misconduct of officials and spectators is to be reported, as well as that of players.*
2. *As incidents happen, do not rely on your memory. Record the time of the incident, as well as any words that were spoken to you and gestures made.*
3. *The referee must act upon the testimony of his neutral linesman, even though the referee may not have seen the incident.*
4. *After the match, incidents must not be discussed, even with other referees. Reports from referees or linesmen must be filed separately, usually within 24 hours.*
5. *All cautions and send offs must be reported. Cite the reasons, and be accurate.*
6. *The referee's report must include all incidents on and off the field.*
7. *When the referee's report has been made and submitted, the assignment has been completed.*

WHEN REFEREES MEET

"Criticism will come from coaches...
if it doesn't first come from our own ranks."

The word "meeting" does not exactly conjure up squeals of delight, whether a person be a businessman, teacher, union member, churchgoer, or referee. Unfortunately for a soccer official it is often that time when referees get together to air grievances, boast about top assignments that were handled with ease, complain about the deterioration of play and conduct of players and to quibble about their *own* interpretations of the Laws of the Game. (Without a rule book, of course.) Many referees are too set in their ways, and their own learning process terminated years ago.

To any serious observer of the game, there is something new to be learned from each assignment. Moreover, the good referee will realize that even a seasoned veteran of international matches will make mistakes, and that the only substantive difference among referees is often the degree and frequency of these mistakes. If a group of referees openly admit that their Referee Association meetings can provide a vehicle for freely admitting mistakes and correcting ignorance, they will find their field efforts improved.

The referee's privileged position in the game must not be taken lightly. His never-ending education is gained through the study of the Laws of the Game, his observation of other referees, game experience, and in communication with fellow referees. Our objective here is to offer some suggestions as to how this communication process can be effected through educational group meetings.

SUGGESTED ACTIVITIES FOR REFEREE MEETINGS
(exclusive of training sessions for new referees)

- **A non-threatening written test** is an excellent method for initiating rules discussion. Since time is valuable, tests should be taken individually and brought to the meeting, having been corrected by the referee. Test scores need not be discussed. Each item should be discussed individually, and new items may be added for future tests.

- **A review of certain Laws of the Game** is advisable, particularly at the beginning of the season. Law XI, Off-Side, and Law XII, Fouls and Misconduct, are the most obvious for generating lively discussion.

- **Audio-visual material** such as videos will aid in clarifying certain points of disagreement. These videos need not necessarily be on the Laws, and may not be directed toward referees, but could be match videos which can be studied from the standpoint of game control and law application.

- **Reviews of books.** A few books now exist on refereeing, and can be reported upon by a member. FIFA News carries interesting and timely information on rule interpretations, and this should be regularly brought to the attention of the association.

- **Outside speakers.** These people may have distinguished themselves in areas outside of refereeing. An accomplished referee or umpire in another sport may also bring new insights into game-control referee education.

- **Game situations.** Each meeting should have at least a short period devoted to recent situations on the field. These situations may be collected and used from year to year as "Case Book" studies.
- **Referee evaluation -- on field.** If time and conditions permit, the group should observe a senior referee in a game, and his performance should be evaluated.
- **Individual contributions by member referees.** In order for maximum efficiency to be achieved within the association, each member must participate actively at least once during the year. Each member should be given a topic for presentation, either in writing or as an instructional device at a meeting. A list of topics for presentation could include:
  - Pre-game instructions from a referee to his linesmen
  - Cooperation between referees and linesmen
  - Dealing with injuries
  - Administering a caution
  - Timing, and when to add time
  - Writing disciplinary reports
  - When is a charge a fair charge?
  - Refereeing with club linesmen
  - How to evaluate a fellow official
  - Dealing with dissent

HINTS
1. *Many times an individual with limited or non-existent refereeing experience can best run your meetings. Like any administrator, he should be able to organize, delegate authority, and bring out the best in the membership.*
2. *Newsletters provide the needed communication during the off-season.*
3. *Try to include at least one social event each year in your calendar of activities. The sacrificing soccer spouse should certainly be included.*
4. *Some referee groups award an annual trophy or award to an outstandingly sportsmanlike player, team, or coach. You may want to recognize one of your own referees.*
5. *Coaches, players, and other administrators should be invited to attend meetings. For obvious reasons, game mistakes and game situations are not to be discussed in their presence.*

There once was a player-coach in a college game during the early years of the game in California. With five minutes remaining in the game, and his team behind, 15-0, the coach shouted to his team after still another score: "Come on, let's give them five good minutes of play." What other scenarios can you imagine in one-sided games, and what is the frequent result in such frustrating circumstances? What can you do to help make such a negative experience a more positive one for both teams?

The ideal referee, in control and aware of all that's around her.

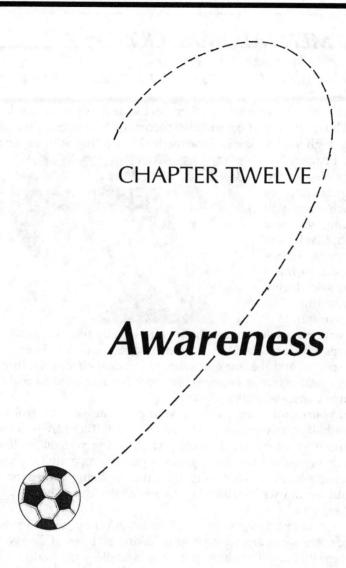

CHAPTER TWELVE

Awareness

*"The referee should bring himself just slightly above
the level of the players.
Close enough so you're experiencing what they are.
Far enough away so you're untouchable
in matters of controversy."*
Source unknown

MENTAL IMAGERY
by Donald L. Wilbur

Donald Wilbur is a former USSF National Referee and a National NISOA Referee.

For those of us who are trying to manage others on the field, we must first learn to manage ourselves. The refereeing of competitive soccer can be a stress-producing event, and it can create high anxiety levels. One method of dealing with anxiety is simply called "mental imagery."

Mental imagery is also called visualization, imagination, or mental rehearsal. Each time you think about something, you are using your imagination, that is, you are using mental imagery. **Think now** of a special person, eating a lemon, or of what was said during your last referee meeting. Did images flash through your mind?

Before making an important telephone call, do you mentally rehearse what you will say? Now, perhaps you can see why mental imagery can be effective. It prepares you for the expected and the unexpected. You can deal effectively, in your head, with a person or event before it happens, before it is confronted in real life, thus helping you become a more effective official.

Imagery will build your confidence, improve your concentration, control your emotional responses, and ultimately enhance your performance. There are two kinds of imagery: external and internal. External imagery is observing yourself as if you were on videotape. Pretend you are watching yourself perform an activity, such as the awarding of a penalty-kick. See not only the attacker being fouled or the deliberate "hands", but your own positioning to make the call. That is... **see yourself as others will see you.**

Internal imagery refers to imagining yourself performing from your own eyes. It should look as if there were a camera on your head taking pictures of everything you would see in a given situation. To use the previous example, you would see the players and the ball in the penalty-area, but you are absent from the picture. Internal imagery is **how you see others.**

Studies have shown that an internal perspective is more effective than the external; a combination of the two is best. It allows you to experience imagery as if you were a performer (internal) and an observer (external). As long as the image is detailed, clear, and controllable, it can be effective.

To fully benefit from mental imagery, you need to relax and concentrate. Focus on a positive performance. Later, you can control the mistakes you often make in a game. Manipulate the images so they do what you want them to do. The closer your images are to the real thing, the better they translate into improved performance. Feel the humidity and the heat; make it real.

COACHES AND REFEREES...
How We See Each Other

Referees soon learn that the attitude of the coach is reflected in the demeanor of the players. Words from the bench are quickly assimilated on the field, immediately followed by a "carrying out" of these instructions or observations.

For the referee, each game and each contact with a coach must be a sincere effort to improve the soccer experience. Consider what others expect of us and what we expect of coaches:

THE IDEAL COACH is one who:
- Respects the neutrality of officials.
- Knows the Laws and instructs players on their observance.
- Considers sport a preparation for life.
- Prepares the team for the unexpected, unwanted, even the unwarranted.
- Applauds efforts over results.
- Accepts disappointment and defeat.

The coach at halftime.

"Without the coach's help, it is almost impossible for the referee to apply the Laws of the Game." - Alfred Kleinaitis, Director of Instruction, USSF

THE IDEAL REFEREE is one who:
- Protects the skilled from the unskilled.
- Understands the frustration of unrewarded effort and preparation.
- Brings out the best in everyone in the game, including partners, players, coaches and spectators.
- Has studied the Laws, refereeing AND the game.

THE PHIELD TEST

Referees, like players, are competitive. A healthy competition, and a test of referees' speed and agility is offered in the PHield Test. It can easily be set up on any open area soccer field. The difference between the slowest and fastest referee in your group should be no more than 15 seconds. Suggesting passing time: 60 seconds.

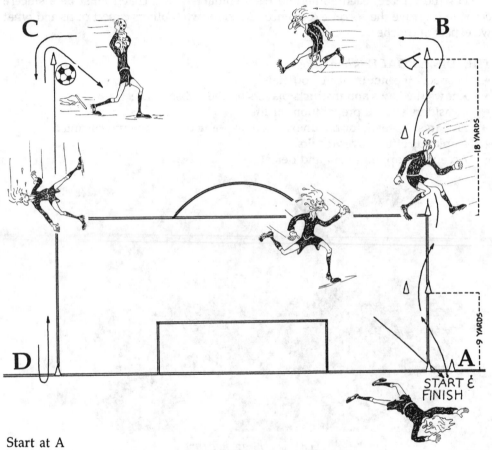

Start at A

A → B	Run backward, weaving through cones, which are one yard apart. (add one second for each cone hit or set of cones missed)
B	Pick up linesman's flag
B → C	PROPERLY carry linesman's flag at a full sprint... either side acceptable
C	Drop flag, pick up ball and make a PROPER throw-in toward the goal
C → D → C	Sideways run, facing penalty-area... do NOT cross feet (add 2 seconds for improper run)
C → A	Sprint to finish... between cones at A

CHALLENGING REFEREES THROUGH GAMES...
Out of the classroom to the field, where real decisions are made.

The classroom has its place for instructing in the Laws, for videos, testing, and for general discussion. Field work, however, is an equal challenge to the instructor and to the referee. In order to maintain interest, field work must confront, probe, educate, and stretch the mental and physical capacities of referees. These activities are for any size group of 15 or more, and require a minimum of organization.

OUT OF BOUNDS
Purpose: Accuracy on judging balls over the touchline.

Participants: Two teams of at least two players each. One "referee" (R), and linesmen.

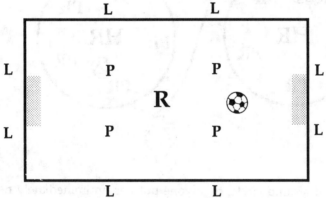

Venue: 20x20 yard field, with goals (pylons) set 3 yards apart on opposite sides of field. Option: Use four goals, with each team attempting to score in opponent's goal(s).

Activity: R runs game, and keeps activity moving. Each time ball goes over one of the four lines, two competing players, one from each team, report to the R as to who last touched the ball. R keeps a record of the result. Anyone may put the ball into play on the throw-in. Linesmen (L) also record their decision on who last touched ball. After 10 "decisions", R announces the answers. Each L should have minimum 80% accuracy. The winning L becomes R for the next series, and some L become players.

Variation: R may instruct L to walk around the periphery while ball is in play. This will take away any advantage a linesman may have due to "one-sided" play and create a more realistic game. You may wish to increase number of players in the small space, making it more difficult for decisions.

CONCENTRATION

Purpose: 1) To develop and to challenge the referee's powers of concentration. 2) To develop peripheral vision, and 3) To develop friendly competitiveness among referees.

Participants: Two Head Referees (HR), one in each circle. Ten Player-Referees (PR), five in each circle. One Active Referee (AR).

Venue: Two circles of PR, about ten yards in diameter. Five yards between circles.

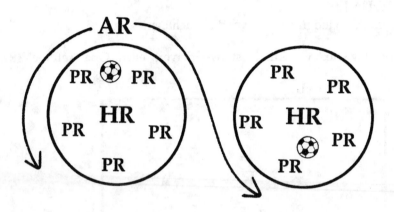

Activity: Ball kicked around circle, to anyone but person immediately next to the kicker. AR moves clockwise around the outside of the two circles. HR counts touches to ball in one sixty second period, and keeps time.

Players can become more active by counting touches (to themselves), and by challenging PR to whom ball is passed. For instance, PR (A) may say, "Law I" as he passes the ball. The recipient, PR (B) must answer by saying "Field of Play".

Variation: If the ball goes out of the circle, everyone must subtract one touch from the total.

At the end of one minute, the AR must have gone around each circle at least three times, and must accurately report the number of touches in both circles.

AR must jog, walk, side-step, or run forward or backward, according to instructions of HR nearest the AR at that times.

Comment: This challenging exercise is much more difficult that it may appear on paper. Few AR's will be able to accurately "count" touches in each circle while listening to movement instructions from HR's. However, each AR will improve his observation skills and peripheral vision.

GIVE THE BALL BACK TO THE PLAYERS...
$5 A MINUTE!
Making It All Worth The Investment
by Tom Mallen

No doubt you know the difference between time wasting and time consumption. Think about the consumption of time and how the re-starts claim a third of of the time in your games.

RESTART*	FREQUENCY	SECONDS	TOTAL
Throw-in	35	12	370
Goal-kick	9	20	180
Corner-kick	7	25	175
Free-kick (including sanctions, off-side)	15	15	270
Penalty-kick	1	45	45
Goals (kick-off)	4	40	160
TOTAL	71		1200 (20 minutes per game)

Tom Mallen is an accountant who has refereed 2000 games and coached 20 teams.

Have you thought about the cost** of putting the two teams on the field?

PLAYER	ANNUAL COST		TEAM	
Registration	$55.00		Banner	$45.00
Shoe	30.00		Refreshments	270.00
Shinguards	15.00		Miscellaneous***	285.00
Ball	10.00			
	$110.00			$600.00

(x 15 = $1,650) + $600 = $2250 per season, or $150 per game

Two teams = $300 per game or

$\longrightarrow$ **$5 A MINUTE**

* Based on a 20 game Fair or Foul? study of 60 minute games.

** Based on a 15 player team and a 15 game season with volunteer referees.

*** Transportation costs, trophies, parties, team photos.

Referees can recognize lost-time situations and use preventive mechanics to maximize playing time. Observe field conditions prior to the game and place ball persons behind goals. Keep the game moving. Avoid interfering with ball positions on free-kicks. Add time for your paperwork on goals scored. Think of ways to allow more playing time. Give the ball back to the players.

Arturo Angeles, the United States referee at the top. Diego Maradona seeks sympathy. "Not all tackles are fouls," responded Angeles. (Argentina-Greece)

CHAPTER THIRTEEN

The World Cup

"What a party. It was a memorable experience for everyone concerned, a gigantic soccer festival with superb sporting standards"...
FIFA booklet on WC '94

THE 1994 WORLD CUP

There were surprises everywhere. The 1994 World Cup may be the standard by which all future World Cups are measured. Never have so many (68,991 average per game) seen so much soccer (62 minutes average playing time per game) in such an atmosphere of clean play (29 fouls per game). More goals were scored than in any previous World Cup, except for Spain in 1982. George Cumming, Development Director of the Scottish Football Association and Member of the International Board, summed up the performance of the referees: "The message to the world was, 'Look what's been accomplished. Now, go back to your countries and apply what you've seen'." Soccer authority Stanley Lover said, "Some of the lost dignity has been put back into the game."

Clearly, FIFA had been distressed and frustrated by Italy '90. The world had seen the fewest goals per game in World Cup history, and the vivid memories of the violent Final would not disappear. Three months before Italy '90, 60% of FIFA's hand-picked referees had failed the physical test in Pisa. It was time for change, and Joseph Blatter, FIFA General Secretary, was given the assignment of changing the image of World Cup soccer. The concerns were as follows:

1. Accurate applications of Law XI would be required. The off-side Law now stated that attackers who were even with the second-to-last defender would not be judged off-side. Specialized linesmen were instructed to flag for off-side only if there was no doubt of a player's field position and participation in play.

2. Superior fitness would be a prime requisite for participation. The 24 referees and 22 linesmen would be monitored as athletes, not only as officials. All were physically well-prepared for the sultry and demanding conditions at all venues. In 1994 the average age for referees was 40 years and 5 months, compared with a much higher average in 1990. FIFA had discovered that Italy '90 had produced a number of games officiated by older referees. Many of these games ended early.

3. Strong actions must be taken against foul play, especially the tackle from behind. With 225 cautions and 15 send-offs, in 1994 no games were seen as violent.

4. An increase in playing time would be sought. In World Cup '94 referees were seen closely monitoring the passage of time on injuries, goal celebrations, and other time-consuming incidents. Injured players were immediately carried off for treatment. Time allowances for the above factors averaged nearly six minutes.

5. Specially trained linesmen would be required. A separate list of FIFA linesmen was created. Teams of officials were carefully chosen, with all having a basic speaking knowledge of English. Their average age was also 40 years and 5 months.

6. The image of soccer referees must change. FIFA emphasized their desire to elevate the position of referees. The new, popular referee shirts have

Never before was a World Cup so closely watched, by so many. Those who instruct candidates, interpret the Laws, and whistle and run line in FIFA's 191 member countries were impressed. While the World Cup was an overwhelming success for all, new problems have arisen. There are challenges that must be met. The soccer world needs to study the 52 games of WC '94 and to seek further change.

1. Shirt-pulling and other holding is a persistent and desperate act by many players. Though it seldom brings on physical injury, it must be strongly discouraged by all referees. (A player who holds an opponent to prevent him from gaining possession of the ball must be cautioned.)

2. The use of the arm for holding off (pushing) opponents is also a problem, particularly by attackers near the opposing goal. Though obvious, it was seldom sanctioned.

3. Player deportment was usually in the interests of fair play. Some players still protested decisions, however, and engaged in ungentlemanly conduct. "Dives" in or near the penalty-area occurred in many games, without cautions.

4. "We think that 80% of injured players are not injured in such a manner that needs immediate treatment. Feigning is cheating", Joseph Blatter (Referee Magazine, March '93). The faking of injuries, possibly the most difficult of all player activity to detect with certainty, needs continued scrutiny.

5. Foot movement by goalkeepers at the taking of penalty-kicks draws attention to the need for a Law change. Flagrant violations were seen in many of these kicks, yet referees continue to allow this unfair advantage taken by the goalkeepers. (The fifteen penalty-kicks were all converted. After overtime, twenty nine kicks from the penalty-mark were attempted. Eighteen went into the goal. Obvious goalkeeper movement of the feet was noted on ten of these kicks.)

6. Referee-linesman cooperation and mechanics problems are always magnified in the World Cup. Many referees are seen calling their own game, with limited attention to linesmen. The linesman was closer to play than the referee in a critical game when there was a "no call" in the penalty area. Should a linesman raise the flag when he is sure the referee is not in position to accurately decide? In this case, justice was not served, though the referee himself later admitted the mistake that could have prevented a team's move to the next round of play.

All of the above are may be lessons for FIFA as they prepare for the 1998 World Cup in France. The differences between your games and the World Cup experience may not be as pronounced as you think. What are the lessons that you can take to your games?

1. Maintain your composure at all times. Consider the referee in Bolivia-Spain, as he "hammers" the ball to the ground for the taking of a penalty-kick. Contrast this with Bulgaria-Italy, as the quietly efficient referee removes himself from the action, supervising the kick from a safe distance.

2. Even at the World Cup, field conditions vary. The Sweden-Romania game was on a hard surface, resulting in higher bounces and a faster roll of the ball. Compare this with the problems of a heavy, soggy turf. Each brings

special challenges to the official. Also, did you notice the "stripes", resulting from the cutting of the grass? These markings help linesmen (offside) and referees (10 yards). Look for similar markings and points of reference at your fields. (Stripes from grass-cutting are helpful to referees and linesmen only if the stripes are parallel to the goal-lines.)

3. Be ready for the unexpected. In Belgium-Germany, the Belgian goalkeeper, later voted the outstanding goalkeeper of the World Cup, left his goal in a desperate attempt to score, fully 120 yards from where you might expect to see him. The world's goalkeepers now have a new idea, and so should the referee!

4. Study the taking of free-kicks. The difference between '90 and '94 is astounding. In '94 encroachment on free-kicks was minimal. When referees found it necessary to mark off the ten yards, players often refused to move. Be consistent, and caution players when they fail to retreat the ten yards.

5. Study the advantage, and how it has helped or has been a negative experience in your games. The "advantage of advantages" led to the only goal in Norway-Mexico. Was it this application of the advantage which earned Sandor Puhl his place in the Final?

A stoppage in play during the World Cup. The ball is being returned from the stands as the referee replaces a divot and the linesman looks into the crowd. During re-starts, be sure to keep all of your attention on the players.

THE HIDDEN "FOUL" OF WORLD CUP '94?

Get out the tape and watch the final two minutes of Belgium-Morocco. It was the unseen "foul" of the World Cup. There was an off-side trap, a flag, then the whistle for off-side. Wait a minute. Off-side is not a foul. Both the attacker Weber and the goalkeeper Azmi ignored the whistle. All alone, travelling almost 25 yards in 2.9 seconds, Weber went for goal. At the top of the penalty-arc, Azmi went for Weber. Azmi's desperate lunge at Weber's upper legs left both players motionless on the ground. Weber had been sent hurtling four feet in the air.

"Red card", "send-off", "violent conduct" have been the responses of referees who saw it. Azmi was carried off, ending a delay of 2 minutes and 43 seconds. All awaited the red card for Azmi, possibly a yellow for Weber, and a free-kick for Morocco near mid-field. The game was re-started at the point of the hidden tackle, for Morocco!

Weber pushes the ball, at top speed, going around Azmi (note ball). Azmi determines only one course of action... forget the ball and stop Weber.
(Computer-generated photo)

LESSONS FOR REFEREES
- *On the off-side, the whistle does not always stop play. You may have to give a very loud whistle <u>and</u> possibly a second whistle if play continues.*
- *Keep your eyes on possible play after the whistle, not on the linesman.*
- *Caution attacking players who continue play after hearing the whistle.*

FINAL WORD: It is very possible that neither linesman nor the referee saw the above incident. If the fourth official saw this violent conduct, is it his duty to report it to the referee? Yes.

USSF Referees
Who Have Participated in the World Cup

1962 - Leo Goldstein   Chile   Line: Chile / Italy
New York   Hungary / England

1970 - Henry Landauer   Mexico   Referee: Sweden / Uruguay
California   Line: USSR / Belgium
                                             Mexico / Belgium
                                           Italy / Mexico

1982 - David Socha   Spain   Referee: Scotland / New Zealand
Massachusetts   Line: Poland / Italy

1986
David Socha   Mexico   Referee: South Korea / Italy
                                     Line: Paraguay / Iraq
                                         Spain / Brazil
                                         Belgium / USSR

1990 - Vincent Mauro   Italy   Referee: Belgium / South Korea
Massachusetts   Line: Argentina / Cameroon
                                           Sweden / Scotland
                                         Belgium / Spain
                                         Germany F.R. / Netherlands
                                         Cameroon / England

1994 - Arturo Angeles   USA   Referee: Argentina / Greece
California

THE STORY BEHIND THE STORY

     In an unusual request, Leo Goldstein implored FIFA to let him take part in the 1962 World Cup. He paid his own expenses, but he had a point to make. Not twenty years before, soccer had saved his life.

     Standing in line at the notorious Dachau extermination camp, he and all around him were being led to the gas chamber. An officer in charge, who was a German international player, recognized Goldstein as one who had whistled games prior to the war. The officer pulled him from the line, indicating his services were needed in the area. Goldstein promised himself that if he lived, he would give back to the game. He became America's first World Cup official, and served soccer for many years in the New York area before succumbing to a heart attack in the late 1980's.

Bulgaria-Germany
<u>THE</u> Off-side Call of World Cup '94?

The closer play is to goal, the more difficult the off-side decisions are for referee and linesman. Why? Because play is frantic, the goalkeeper may have moved off of the goal-line, and intense activity brings players together in attacking and defending the goal. Furthermore, a linesman's view may be obstructed.

In the 73rd minute of Bulgaria-Germany, an unusual off-side occurred, and the referee was equal to the challenge. It may have been the best off-side call of WC '94.

When the 21 yard shot was taken by Moeller (A-M), attacker Voeller (A-V) was in an off-side position.

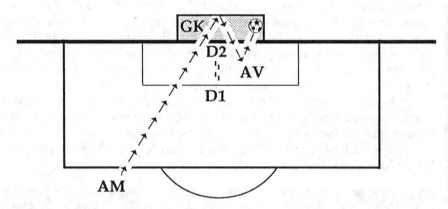

When he received the ball directly from the crossbar, Voeller was in an on-side position, because the defender had moved from D^1 to D^2. Voeller was immediately judged off-side because the ball was last played by A-M, a player of A-V's side and when it was played, A-M was in front of the ball and did not have at least two opponents between himself and the goal-line. Though the play (AM shot, to crossbar, to AV, to goal) consumed a fraction of a second, the decision was immediately and correctly made.

LESSONS FOR REFEREES AND LINESMEN

1. *Just before an attacker shoots at goal, glance to the penalty-area and/or goal-area for attacker(s) off-side position.*
2. *Be quick about your decision, for attacks on goal often result from off-side positions.*

This example appears in the instructional video on "Off-side" available for viewing through USSF's Clinicians, State Referee Administrators and AYSO's Director of Instruction.

ARTURO ANGELES
U.S. Soccer's Referee Representative to WC '94

"Today's referees must promote fair play and make the game more attractive to players and fans."

Tears came to the eyes of Arturo Angeles' family, watching 3000 miles away as he fulfilled the dream of many referees... whistling a game in the World Cup, in one's own country. Arturo has vivid recollections of the game, from the coin toss in which the world's most recognized player said "Heads" until the penalty-kick in the last minute of a one-sided game between Argentina and Greece.

Arturo is a veteran of 100 international games, but his 90 minutes in the sun and humidity at Foxboro Stadium near Boston is the highlight of his 24 years with the whistle. It was, as the famed soccer broadcaster Andres Cantor exclaimed, "La Clima Enorme (The highest pinnacle). I can still hear the FIFA anthem, the sheer brilliance of the occasion and the crowd as they cheered us at halftime", said the civil engineer and former goalkeeper. "It was a referee's dream". The pressures were tremendous. Arturo represented the United States well, and his handling of the game earned him an 8.5 on the FIFA rating scale of 10.

In his intense preparation for the World Cup, the always soft-spoken Angeles must have had flashbacks to highlights of a very rewarding career. Whistling in local leagues for four years before becoming a 20 year veteran USSF referee, Angeles was seasoned for the task before him. He had been to the Olympics, the U.S. Cup '93, and the Copa America.

At a Cup semi-final in Southern California, Arturo administers the penalty-kick.

Some will be surprised to find that Arturo considers the Sunday leagues, where he started his career, as the most difficult to control. "In international soccer, you must keep things going. No one comes to see the referee perform. The proper use of advantage is just one way of serving the game by NOT calling a foul. In local leagues, however, there are many frustrated players. They'll get very upset if you play the advantage, and will often stop after the foul. They seem satisfied with the foul, though the awarding of the foul often accomplishes nothing. It's not that we're there to satisfy players, but you must always remember the skill level and expectations of players."

WORDS OF ADVICE FROM ARTURO ANGELES

Make sure your control of the game doesn't interfere with the skills of players. Take on the responsibility of making the game attractive for everyone.

Stay fit by learning to train properly. (Note: Angeles joined a running club to develop speed and stamina.)

Mental stamina is a requirement. Learn to deal with all kinds of pressures that are put upon you.

Never give up. "There was violence directed at me twice in my first four games, and again in my first amateur game wearing the FIFA patch. (FIFA referees are required to wear the FIFA patch in every game they officiate, regardless of the level of play.) I took all of this in stride. I immediately studied the mechanics and game control techniques of top referees, and this helped me through this process."

Be flexible. "Once I had to do a game by myself for the first half, with 60,000 fans watching. One linesman had failed to show, and someone sent him out to find another linesman. Neither showed until halftime! Think about how you would handle such a situation. You must be prepared for anything."

As you are promoted through the ranks, learn to communicate with everyone. Be noticeable, and seek help any place you can find it.

Arturo has never watched the videotape of his World Cup game. He much prefers to talk about the future, and to broaden his contributions to soccer. He now writes a regular column for a Spanish language newspaper, and wants to continue instructing other referees. "I enjoyed my games", and wrote FIFA and told them this. "It was something I'll always carry with me."

Arturo was also the fourth official in three games: Italy-Ireland, Korea-Germany, and Spain-Switzerland.

SPECIAL THANKS TO A BENEVOLENT FRIEND
BILL MASON
SOCCER'S FRIEND... EVERYONE'S FRIEND

Almost ten years ago, we recognized Bill Mason's superlative knowledge of the Laws, making the bold statement that he "could have written them himself." This declaration still stands and is confirmed by no less an expert than Ken Aston, who recently wrote: "As a Law interpreter, he is second to none anywhere in the world."

With more than 25 years' service to AYSO (including eleven years as a coach) and for the last several years AYSO's representative on the United States Soccer Federation Referee Committee, Bill's benevolence to the game seems unending. A USSF State Referee Instructor and an AYSO National Instructor, Bill is a keen observer, not only of the Laws, but of referees as well. He has been at the forefront of changes at AYSO, and continues to serve on the Referee Commission.

Bill has helped in editing, research, and re-writing this sixth edition; this assistance comes not only to aid friends, but to help the game itself and those charged with the responsibility of refereeing. Two of his trademarks, the multicolored pens and his gentle professionalism, have assisted us greatly in this edition, at a time when others were also seeking his wisdom. Thank you, Bill.

Bill Mason (left) with Ken Aston. Through his foresight and determination, Bill encouraged Aston to become an active participant in the training, development, and retention of AYSO's referees. They both agree that the referee's education never ends.

CHAPTER FOURTEEN

Appendices...
For those who want to know more.

*"We must accept authority in a way
that is self-disciplined."*
Source unknown

GLOSSARY, DEFINITIONS, AND TERMS

AYSO - The American Youth Soccer Organization, a national affiliate member of the United States Soccer Federation.

Bicycle-kick - An over-the-head kick, often used in an attempt on goal.

Caution - An official disciplinary action by the referee to a player who (a) persistently infringes the Laws of the Game, (b) shows dissent by word or action from any decision given by the referee, (c) is guilty of ungentlemanly conduct or, (d) enters or re-enters or leaves the field without the permission of the referee.

Charging - Bodily contact, usually consisting of one shoulder against another shoulder. A charge may be fair or foul.

Club Linesman - A linesman with a flag who has been appointed by the referee to indicate out of bounds balls and the direction of the throw-in, subject to the decision of the referee. He is usually a club official or supporter.

Continental Federations - There are six Continental Federations under the direction of FIFA. They are: (1) Confederacion Norte-Centroamericana y del Caribe de Futbol (CONCACAF); (2) Confederacion Sudamericana de Futbol (CONMEBOL) ; (3) Asian Football Confederation (AFC); (4) Union of European Football Association (UEFA); (5) Oceania Football Confederation (OFC) (Oceania); (6) Confederation Africaine de Football (AFRICA).

Dead Ball - The ball is dead whenever it is not in play. This occurs when the ball is outside of the field of play or due to any temporary suspension of the game due to an infringement of the rules or when the game is otherwise stopped by the referee.

Deliberate foul - The world "deliberate" is used only in relation to the "hand" ball, which must be judged "deliberate" before being called by the referee.

Diagonal System - The internationally recognized system of game control, involving a referee and two neutral linesmen.

Direct Free-Kick - A free-kick awarded when an opponent has committed one of the ten penal offenses. A goal may be scored directly into an opponents' goal.

Double-Kick - See Scissor-Kick.

Drop-Ball - A ball which is dropped on the field by the referee after he has stopped the game due to an injury, foreign object on the field, or due to a similar circumstance when no breach of the laws has occurred.

Dual System - The method of control sometimes called the Two Referee System of Control, where two referees of equal authority are on the field of play. This system is no longer favored by most soccer referees or organizations.

End-line - The entire goal-line from touch-line to touch-line.

FIFA - The Federation Internationale de Football Association, which is the international governing body of soccer. Address: FIFA, Hitzigweg 11, 8030 Zurich, Switzerland.

Formations - The lining up of players into certain prescribed locations on the field, according to style of play and team objectives. The goalkeeper is not mentioned in formation discussions, for his is the only fixed position on the field. Players located immediately in front of the goalkeeper are listed first. The most common formations are 4-2-4, and 4-3-3. Referees should know a team's basic formation, particularly with regard to judging the off-side.

Forwards - The front line of a team.

Free-Kick - An unchallenged kick in any direction. It is awarded for an infringement by the opposing side.

Indirect... A goal may not be scored directly.

Direct... A goal may be scored directly into the opponents' goal.

Fullbacks - Players who form the defense in front of the goalkeeper.

Goal - (a) That area between the upright posts and under the cross-bar, (b) the two posts and the cross-bar themselves, (c) the unit of scoring. A ball passing completely over the goal-line and in the area termed "goal" is a "goal."

Goal-Kick - The kick that puts the ball in play after it has gone over the goal-line of the defense and was last touched by a member of the attacking team. A goal-kick is not in play until it has passed out of the penalty-area.

Goalkeeper (goalie) - Sometimes called "goaldie" by seven year olds just beginning soccer. The player who guards the goal. He may use his hands within his own penalty-area. He has all the privileges of every other player on the field, plus a few of his own.

Goal-Line - The end-line (width of the field) which extends from touch-line to touch-line, passing directly under the cross-bar of the goal.

Goal-Mouth - That area immediately in front of the goal.

Going Over the Ball - The practice of raising one's foot above and over the ball in such a manner that when the opponent attempts to kick the ball, he is likely to be cleated in the shin. This is "kicking" an opponent, a penal offense, which results in a direct free-kick or a penalty-kick..

Halfbacks - The middle line of a team. The first line of defense, or the second line of attack.

Halfway-Line - The line in the center of the field extending from touch-line to touch-line and dividing the field into two equal parts.

Hand-Ball - A ball touching the hand or arm of any player with the exception of the goalkeeper within his own penalty-area. The player must have deliberately moved the hand toward the ball, or must have been carrying the hand or arm in an unnatural position in order for the "hands" to be called.

Hidden fouls - Those fouls that usually go undetected by the referee, and are therefore unpunished. They are usually committed by experienced players and can cause unpleasant incidents in a game.

Holding - Grasping an opponent or an opponent's uniform.

Indirect Free-Kick - A free-kick from which a goal may not be scored directly.

Inswinger - a term used in conjunction with a corner-kick which hooks in toward the goal. (See outswinger)

Kick-Off - A kick from the center of the field to put the ball in play at the start of each period and after each score. (Also called place-kick.)

Laws of Soccer - The rules of the game, as established by The International Football Association Board and published annually by FIFA. There are 17 Laws of the Game.

FAIR OR FOUL?

Law 18 - An unwritten "law" sometimes used rather blatantly by referees to justify any type of decision which deviates from the Laws of soccer, International Board rulings, or common interpretations. It should be viewed as a common sense law pertaining only to those aspects and situations of the game not previously documented.

Modified Diagonal System - A system of game control which has won favor with many referees, coaches, and players. It places a referee and two line referees on the field, each with a whistle. It is generally acknowledged that fewer fouls result from this system.

Neutral Linesman - A fully qualified game official who is assigned to act as linesman on the diagonal system of control.

Obstruction - The action of one player as he impedes the progress of an opponent's movement on the field. It is sanctioned by an indirect free-kick. When the ball is within playing distance of the player who obstructs, the obstruction is legal.

Off-side - being judged illegally in advance of the ball.

Off-side Position - Being in advance of the ball, but not sanctioned by the referee. Usually, this is due to a player's not taking advantage of this off-side position. It is not a violation of the Laws to be in an off-side position.

Off-side Trap - Fullbacks deliberately moving forward to put an opposing forward in an off-side position. Also called "the Hungarian off-side"; this is legal.

Outswinger - A term used in conjunction with a corner-kick which hooks out and away from the goal toward the center of the field. (See inswinger.)

Pass - To kick, head, or otherwise play the ball intentionally to a teammate.

Penalty-Area - The 18 x 44 yard rectangular area in front of each goal, in which the goalkeeper may touch the ball. Any defensive action committed in this area which would have resulted in a direct free-kick if committed elsewhere results in a penalty-kick.

Penalty-Kick - An unchallenged kick taken by the attacking team from a spot 12 yards from the goal-line. All attacking players except the kicker must be behind the penalty-mark and outside of the penalty-area and behind the penalty-mark. The goalkeeper, who must stand on the goal-line between the posts, is the only defensive player allowed in the penalty-area until the ball has been put in play (traveled its circumference) by the kicker.

Periods - The halves of a game.

Playing Distance - That distance between the player and the ball that would allow the player to reach out with a part of his body (usually his foot) and play the ball.

Pushing - Use of the hands or body to move an opponent. One of the penal offenses.

Quarter Circle - The corner-area, from which corner-kicks are taken.

Referee - The appointed official in charge of a game.

Sandwiching - Two teammates converging simultaneously on an opponent. This type of "boxing in" is penalized with a direct free-kick.

Save - A move by the goalkeeper that prevents a goal being scored.

Sending Off - The expulsion of a player from a game (red card). It is an official disciplinary action by the referee to a player who (a) is guilty of violent conduct, (b) is guilty of serious foul play, (c) uses foul or abusive language, or (d) is guilty of a second cautionable offense after having received a caution.

Senior Linesman - Designated by the referee, the linesman who will take over for the referee if needed.

Short Corner - Making a quick pass instead of a long cross toward the goal when taking a corner-kick.

Spitting - To eject saliva from the mouth, especially naughty when directed towards another player or a game official. One of the penal fouls, punishable by a severe beating by the mothers watching on the sidelines.

Strikers - The two inside forwards in a 3-3-4 attack.

Sweeper (sometimes called stopper) - The last player in the defense, except for the goalkeeper, as designated by the coach or players. Some of the duties of this person involve organizing the defense and "picking up" loose balls or opponents near the defensive goal.

Touch - That space outside of the field of play, separated from it by the touch-lines.

Touch-lines- The side-lines traveling the length of the field on both sides of the field which extend from goal-line to goal-line.

Tripping - Throwing an opponent by use of the legs, or by other means..

USSF - The United States Soccer Federation, the governing body of soccer in the United States.

Violent Conduct - Intentional rough play which should carry both technical and disciplinary sanctions at the same time.

Volley - To kick a ball before it bounces.

Warning - A "soft caution" given by the referee to a player who is guilty of some infringement of the laws. If the infringement is repeated, a caution (yellow card) usually results.

Now that you've read this far, and think you know it all, don't recite it all to the players and coaches. If you do, be prepared for this reaction.

BOOKS
FOR
REFEREES

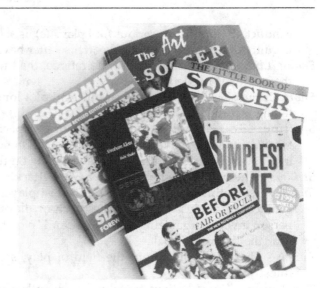

Catlin, Mark
THE ART OF SOCCER - A Better Way to Play
216 pages
> An excellent coaching book, but also for referees who want to understand more about the game and tactics.

Available through Soccer Books, Box 4756-01, St. Paul, MN 55104

Cumming George, Development Director, Scottish Football Association.
FOOTBALL RULES
> This complete package includes a 70 minute video on the basics of the game: The Factual Laws, Authority, The Ball in Play, The Technical Laws, and Restarting the Game, The Fourth Official and Kicks from the Penalty-Mark. Contains overhead transparency master sheets, quiz books and booklets for both instructor and the student. An excellent total package by an expert on the Laws.

Available from: The Scottish Football Association, 6 Park Gardens,
Glasgow, Scotland G3 74F
Tel: 141-332-6372 • Fax: 141-332-7559
Price: $200.00 includes postage & handling from the U.K.

LAWS OF THE GAME (Federation Internationale de Football Association - FIFA)
Printed annually
> Available through the United States Soccer Federation, 1811 South Prairie Avenue, Chicago, IL 60616

Gardner, Paul
THE SIMPLEST GAME
323 pages, published by Macmillan & Company, 1994
> A very readable guide to the world of soccer, including the World Cup.
> Read the 50 pages on tactics, then read it again. It will give you a seasoned and mature knowledge of what happens on the field.

Harris, Paul
BEFORE FAIR OR FOUL - The New Referee's Companion
48 pages, published by Soccer for Americans
> A basic and friendly approach to what's really important to the beginner. This should get anyone through his or her first 10 games. Then, hopefully, they're on their way!

Harris, Paul and Harris, Larry
FAIR OR FOUL - The Complete Guide to Soccer Officiating - Sixth Edition, 1995
> *You have it in your hands. Write and tell us what you think.*

Harris, Paul
THE LITTLE BOOK OF SOCCER -
Everyone's Illustrated Guide to the Laws of the Game.
48 pages, published by Soccer for Americans.
> A favorite of coaches and new referees.

Klein, Abraham and Shalov, Rubi as told to Paul Harris
THE REFEREE'S REFEREE - Becoming the Best
104 pages
> A leading World Cup referee shares many secrets of game control, understanding the game, and with new and solid information on mental and physical preparation.

Lover, Stanley
SOCCER MATCH CONTROL
256 pages, published by Pelham Books, London 1986
> A very comprehensive treatment of the role of the referee, and how to make sure things go "your way".

Mason, Bill and Maisner, Larry
THE RULES OF SOCCER: SIMPLIFIED
24 pages, revised annually.
> Everything that's important about the Laws is contained in this handy booklet. Presents the "must knows", the "should knows" and many of the "could knows" in a thorough but simplified and easily readable manner.

Available through Soccer Learning Systems (non-AYSO sales) - 1-800-762-2376 or Youth Sports Publishing (AYSO edition) - 1-800-297-6386

All books available from Soccer for Americans, except where noted. Write or call for catalog.

SOCCER FOR AMERICANS
Box 836
Manhattan Beach, CA 90266
(310) 372-9000

VIDEOS FOR REFEREES

A HISTORY OF REFEREEING
32 minutes

> An inspirational history of those who have preceded us. From the "mastro de campo" (master of the field) to the modern game.
>
> Brizio Carter of Mexico is shown smiling his way through a very difficult game. "There's about to be a referee's revolution" we are told.
>
> Great for opening up your season at the first referee get-together.

REGIONAL REFEREE VIDEO FIELD GUIDE
29 minutes
produced by the American Youth Soccer Organization

> The best introduction to refereeing basics, presented in a friendly, open and positive way. Also ask for the Regional Referee Field Guide Workbook.

Available through Youth Sports Publishing - 1-800-297-6386

THE ROLE OF THE REFEREE and FITNESS TRAINING FOR REFEREES
Two parts - 50 minutes total
by Ken Ridden of the Football Association (England)

> All aspects of the referee's duties are artfully addressed, including appearance, signals, stoppages, linesman cooperation, application of the Laws, positioning and movement, and control and authority.
>
> The fitness section details the rigors of fitness training and testing.

USE OF THE PENALTY MARK and JUDGING CHALLENGES
Two parts - 56 minutes total
by Ken Ridden of the Football Association (England)

> The *Penalty-Kick* portion provides close detail of all aspects of the penalty-kick, much from the 1990 World Cup.
>
> *Judging Challenges* presents 40 game challenges, providing the viewer with excellent "on-the-field" examples.

SOCCER REFEREEING - Tape #1
50 minutes
by Ken Ridden of the Football Association (England)
From English First Division games. Many examples of fair and unfair challenges.
The referee is given much golden advice about the handling of free-kicks, penalty-kicks and corner-kicks.

SOCCER REFEREEING - Tape #2
50 minutes
by Ken Ridden of the Football Association (England)
Dealing with unsporting behavior. "If you don't do your job, soccer will be the ultimate loser," we are wisely told.
Persistent infringement, ungentlemanly conduct, violent conduct, and serious foul play are shown under real match conditions. Positioning and movement segments are helpful with referee-linesman cooperation.

SOCCER RULES - A Guide to the Laws of the Game
60 minutes
produced and directed by George Cumming, Development Director,
Scottish Football Association
from Football Rules (see Books for Referees)
Gives vivid examples with game footage, much from Scottish soccer. Many incidents from 1990 World Cup.
"First and foremost, soccer is a sport," we are reminded. Excellent survey of all of soccer's Laws, presented by an expert of experts.

UNITED STATES SOCCER FEDERATION
Set of three - 20 minutes each
These videos are not for sale, and may not be copied or reproduced. They may be seen by arrangement through USSF State Directors of Instruction or State Referee Administrators. Contact USSF, 1811 S. Prairie Avenue, Chicago, IL 60616.
Based on incidents in the 1994 World Cup, the USSF has produced these new videos.
(1) The Off-Side
(2) Dealing with Foul Play
(3) Gamesmanship and Other Trickery

All videos available from Soccer for Americans, except where noted. Write for catalog.

SOCCER FOR AMERICANS
Box 836
Manhattan Beach, CA 90266
(310) 372-9000

A PASSION FOR THE GAME
Futbolisticamente!!!

Some referees are interested only in the youth, preferring to referee only at that level. Others strive for higher and higher levels of play. Many are caught up in the world's passion for soccer. No one was more visible during World Cup '94 than Andres Cantor, the earnest and spirited announcer who provided the play-by-play commentary for all 52 games. Who could forget his

GOOOOOOOOOAL!

after each score? Who would fail to be dazzled by his quick and accurate recognition of every player, while viewing all the games in a television studio? Millions who knew little or no Spanish would feel comfortable, yet excited, as he was brought into everyone's living room.

Futbolisticamente, (no direct English translation, but it loosely means "thinking, being, and existing in the world of soccer-football), we think of Andres and his passion, knowledge, and excitement over the game. When you referee your next game, consider Andres and his role. You too have a role. Give it everything, just like Andres.

BEFORE YOU ACCEPT
THAT NEXT ASSIGNMENT...
ARE YOU READY FOR THIS?

In *"Hamlets"*, a history of the Sutton Fuller Hamlets (Massachusetts) soccer club, Martyn Bowden writes of a most unusual situation regarding referees' competence. After words from the side-line, the author and his assistant were both told to leave the area. Coach Bowden was given a choice, according to League rules: 1) Leave the area, or 2) Take the team off the field, with no penalty, and PLAY THE GAME AGAIN!*

*A team had a right to withdraw from competition if they felt the refereeing favored the home side.

INDEX

INDEX

INDEX

FINAL THOUGHTS:

You are standing on the shoulders of all who have gone before you. The "beautiful game" depends on that tradition, and on your understanding of the principles of sportsmanship and fair play.

Referee to bring yourself *just above* the level of the players.

Be close enough so you're experiencing what they are, yet far enough away so that you are untouchable in all matters of controversy.

IN MEMORIAM

"JIMMY" WALDER (centered above)
"Know the game, keep fit, and conduct yourself as an official."

REFEREEING CAREER • 1909 - 1969
4,500 games • 30,000 miles of running
No yellow cards, no red... they weren't in use then.

A TEST...
If You Think You Know The Laws Of Soccer.

1. Describe Law V, IBD 8.
2. The 1995 Law changes now name which of the 10 penal fouls as "deliberate"?
3. What is a place-kick, and where is it described?
4. Name the accepted shapes and colors of the goalposts.
5. Which law contains information on the players' numbers on the jersey?
6. Which law contains no decisions of the International Board?
7. Under Law VI, who is responsible for suppling the linesmen's flags, the linesmen or the referee?
8. Where may substitutes and substituted players enter and leave the field of play?
9. In which Law does the linesman and his duties in relation to the off-side occur?
10. When may players take refreshments during a match?

Answers below:

10. *Players may take refreshments only during a stoppage of the match, and only on the touchline. Goalkeepers appear to have special treatment, as they often have refreshments in a container near the goal and may take their refreshments at will.*

9. *No law specifically refers to the linesmen and their off-side duties. Law VI, IBD 1 indicates that the linesmen, when neutral, shall draw the referee's attention to any breaches of the Laws of the Game.*

8. *Entry must be at the half-way line, but a player may leave at the nearest point on the field.*

7. *Neither one. The home club is to supply the flags. We understand that somewhere in the world this may occur, but haven't found where this is.*

6. *Law XVII, Corner-Kick.*

5. *There is nothing in the Laws which mentions the numbers on players' jerseys.*

4. *The goalposts may be square, rectangular, round, half-round, or elliptical, and must be white.*

3. *A place-kick is a kick-off, and is described in Law VIII.*

2. *When a player handles the ball.*

1. *This important decision urges the referee to interfere as little as possible in the game, and that small and insignificant offenses shall not be penalized.*

We're sorry about these nasty questions. We hope it accomplished the same for you that it did for us... a little digging through the Laws we thought we knew so well.